Stepping up to the Second Year at University

Programmes in higher education tend to focus attention on the student's first year (because of concerns about student transition and retention) and on their final year (because of students exiting for their future careers). The middle year(s) of programmes receive relatively little attention, which can often lead to a slump in student development at a crucial point in their studies. *Stepping up to the Second Year at University* provides practical advice that can be implemented by staff throughout higher education institutions. Rather than providing a set of prescriptions to be slavishly implemented, it prompts practitioners to think constructively about curriculum design and delivery, and about maximising student potential within the context of their particular institution. Among the questions asked in this book are the following:

- In what way do students' perceptions of their experience shift as they progress through the first two years of study?
- How do psychological factors bear on student engagement and performance in the second year?
- What in the second-year curriculum might need greater attention?
- How can the analysis of institutional data help?

This book builds on critiques of existing international research on the mid-years experience and also features evidence from a significant new research project from Liverpool John Moores University (LJMU). It also provides a number of starting points for institutions' enhancement activities as they seek to make the experience of their students as rewarding as possible. It is a must read for institutional managers of higher academic programmes, higher education practitioners and anyone interested in the development of teaching at higher education level.

Clare Milsom is Director, Teaching and Learning Academy at LJMU.

Martyn Stewart is Senior Lecturer in Research Methods at Liverpool School of Tropical Medicine.

Mantz Yorke is a member of the Project Team at LJMU and is currently Visiting Professor in the Department of Educational Research, Lancaster University.

Elena Zaitseva is a research officer at LJMU.

The Society for Research into Higher Education (SRHE) is an independent and financially self-supporting international learned Society. It is concerned to advance understanding of higher education, especially through the insights, perspectives and knowledge offered by systematic research and scholarship.

The Society's primary role is to improve the quality of higher education through facilitating knowledge exchange, discourse and publication of research. SRHE members are worldwide and the Society is an NGO in operational relations with UNESCO.

The Society has a wide set of aims and objectives. Amongst its many activities the Society:

• is a specialist publisher of higher education research, journals and books, amongst them Studies in Higher Education, Higher Education Quarterly, Research into Higher Education Abstracts and a long running monograph book series.

The Society also publishes a number of in-house guides and produces a specialist series "Issues in Postgraduate Education".

• funds and supports a large number of special interest networks for researchers and practitioners working in higher education from every discipline. These networks are open to all and offer a range of topical seminars, workshops and other events throughout the year ensuring the Society is in touch with all current research knowledge.

• runs the largest annual UK-based higher education research conference and parallel conference for postgraduate and newer researchers. This is attended by researchers from over 35 countries and showcases current research across every aspect of higher education.

SRHE *Society for Research into Higher Education*
Advancing knowledge Informing policy Enhancing practice

73 Collier Street
London N1 9BE
United Kingdom

T +44 (0)20 7427 2350
F +44 (0)20 7278 1135
E srheoffice@srhe.ac.uk

www.srhe.ac.uk

Director: Helen Perkins
Registered Charity No. 313850
Company No.00868820
Limited by Guarantee
Registered office as above

Society for Research into Higher Education (SRHE) series

Series Editor: Jennifer M. Case, University of Cape Town
                 Jeroen Huisman, University of Ghent

Published titles:

Intellectual Leadership in Higher Education: Renewing the Role of the University Professor
Bruce Macfarlane

Strategic Curriculum Change: Global Trends in Universities
Paul Blackmore and Camille B. Kandiko

Reconstructing Identities in Higher Education: The Rise of 'Third Space' Professionals
Celia Whitchurch

The University in Dissent: Scholarship in the Corporate University
Gary Rolfe

Everything for Sale? The Marketisation of UK Higher Education
Roger Brown with Helen Carasso

Literacy in the Digital University: Critical Perspectives on Learning, Scholarship and Technology
Robin Goodfellow and Mary R. Lea

Researching Student Learning in Higher Education: A Social Realist Approach
Jennifer M. Case

Women Leaders in Higher Education: Shattering the Myths
Tanya Fitzgerald

Writing in Social Spaces: A Social Processes Approach to Academic Writing
Rowena Murray

Digital Technology and the Contemporary University: Degrees of Digitization
Neil Selwyn

Stepping up to the Second Year at University: Academic, Psychological and Social Dimensions
Edited by Clare Milsom, Martyn Stewart, Mantz Yorke and Elena Zaitseva

Tables

Boxes

Contributors

Sue Darwent worked as an educational researcher at Liverpool John Moores University (LJMU). Her current research interests concern student retention, the first- and second-year experience and the effect of individual differences on attrition and success.

Peter Hoekstra is Institutional Research Coordinator at the University of Amsterdam. Peter is one of the founders of the Dutch Association for Institutional Research (DAIR) and member of the Executive Committee of the European Association for Institutional Research (EAIR).

Clare Milsom is Director, Teaching and Learning Academy at LJMU. Clare has published papers on student evaluation and is a National Teaching Fellow.

Martyn Stewart is Senior Lecturer in Research Methods at Liverpool School of Tropical Medicine. Martyn has published educational research in student engagement patterns, learning theory, concept mapping and the professional development of lecturers.

Sue Thompson is former Director of Learning and Teaching and Emeritus Professor of Academic Development at LJMU and a National Teaching Fellow.

Wayne Turnbull works in Academic Registry at LJMU. He has published research papers on national credit frameworks and degree classification.

Mantz Yorke is a member of the Project Team at LJMU and is currently Visiting Professor in the Department of Educational Research, Lancaster University. He has published widely on higher education, focusing particularly on 'the student experience'.

Elena Zaitseva is a research officer at LJMU. She has published research papers and book chapters on various aspects of student and staff experience, including collaborative and peer learning, learner transitions and meaning of student feedback.

Series editors' introduction

This series, co-published by the Society for Research into Higher Education and Routledge Books, aims to provide, in an accessible manner, cutting-edge scholarly thinking and inquiry that reflects the rapidly changing world of higher education, examined in a global context.

Encompassing topics of wide international relevance, the series includes every aspect of the international higher education research agenda, from strategic policy formulation and impact to pragmatic advice on best practice in the field. Each book in the series aims to meet at least one of the principle aims of the Society: to advance knowledge; to enhance practice; to inform policy.

This volume edited by Clare Milsom, Martyn Stewart, Mantz Yorke and Elena Zaitseva puts the spotlight on a hitherto relatively neglected arena of research on student learning: the second year of the undergraduate programme. Although many institutions have noted a decline in student performance at this point, it is the first year with its transitional issues from school to higher education, and the final year with its focus on graduateness that have largely held the attention of researchers and academic developers. Based on an extensive case study in a post-1992 UK university, the authors explore various dimensions of the student experience of the second year: academic, social and psychological. This provides a rich and compelling perspective of why 'stepping up to second year' is so challenging. Importantly, the book also includes very practical implications of these research findings, with suggestions for interventions at all levels of the institution.

Jennifer M. Case
Jeroen Huisman

Preface

While there has been significant research into the experience of students in their first year of university, studies focusing on the second year are limited. This book is based on the findings of the first substantive investigation into the second-year experience at a UK university. Titled 'The Forgotten Year? Tackling the Second Year Slump', this research project, which was supported by the Higher Education Academy, aimed to explore patterns of student performance and engagement in the second year. To enable as complete a picture as possible to be developed of this period of study, established institutional datasets were examined and a qualitative exploration of the perspectives of academics, support staff and students was undertaken. What emerged was a rich, complex picture of the student experience at this pivotal stage in their university life cycle. This book describes our findings and suggests possible interventions to promote student engagement and success in their second year of study.

Initially, we felt that the second year was 'forgotten', the strong academic identities associated with the first and final years casting their shadows across the middle year. However, as our research progressed, we realised that rather than it being an aspect of neglect, the defining characteristic of this period of study was the 'step up' from the first to the second year, hence the title of our book. The academic, social and psychological dimensions associated with this stepping up are described from different angles in its chapters. We feel that this book will be of use to all staff working in higher education, senior managers, programme leaders, lecturers, staff in learning and other professional support roles, and student unions. In particular, we consider that this book would be of value to academics engaged in curriculum design and to new lecturers undertaking initial training or accredited programmes in learning and teaching. We expect that some of our findings will be familiar to our readers and will reflect aspects of the student experience in their own institution. Other outcomes and approaches may be new. Our hope is that readers from every higher education context will be able to apply some of our research findings and recommendations to enhance the second-year experience of their students.

Each chapter describes the second year from a particular perspective and is evidenced by different data sources and methodological approaches. In the first chapter, we discuss how student record data revealed a 'slump' in student performance in some second-year programmes. The causes of this performance dip are investigated and suggestions made for improvements to the second year from a policy and practice perspective. Chapter 2 discusses the tensions between quality frameworks that suggest a mostly linear academic progression through an undergraduate degree programme and models of learning that are essentially spiral in nature with learning behaviours developed, reinforced and practised at multiple points within an undergraduate curriculum. In Chapter 3, the shifting of student perspectives from the first to the second year is explored. Also described in this chapter is a methodology for the investigation of large textual datasets. This approach enables more time-effective and systematic qualitative data analysis and interpretation. A quantitative approach to the perspective shift is taken in Chapter 4, with the focus narrowing to look at students' psychological dispositions and the measure of their variation at different stages of the degree. The following two chapters draw on focus group discussion, as well as outcomes of discipline-based projects to support the findings. Chapter 5 is structured into 'problems and potential solutions' with the intention of providing practical suggestions to curriculum developers, and learner support for second-year students is examined specifically in Chapter 6. Chapter 7 draws together the array of institutional databases referred to in preceding chapters and describes the concept of a 'data warehouse' by presenting a case study of the University of Amsterdam. In the final chapter, the research outcomes are drawn together and institutional attitudes and cultures are explored in the context of taking an evidence-based approach to policy development in order to increase institutional effectiveness.

Our multifaceted approaches and innovative use of data have meant that through the course of the project we have been on a truly developmental research journey. We started from a performance-orientated focus that has over time shifted to a student experience and psychology-related discourse. Writing this book has helped us to develop our methodological views and perspectives. We are indebted to staff, students and alumni at Liverpool John Moores University, the case study institution, and their involvement as 'action researchers', research participants and second-year ambassadors. All have been an inspiration to us and shown outstanding dedication to the enhancement of the student experience.

Acknowledgements

This project is the result of a National Teaching Fellowship Scheme initiative funded by the Higher Education Funding Council for England (HEFCE) and managed by the Higher Education Academy.

We would like to acknowledge the following staff, students and alumni of Liverpool John Moores University for their input to, and support of, the project: Simon Brooman, Stevie Cavanagh, Jack Dunne, Andy Flatman, Peter Jago, David McIlroy, Karen Poole, John Rae, Ester Ragonese and Margaret Williams.

We are also grateful to external colleagues, in particular Peter Hoekstra, for generously sharing their approaches to improving engagement and performance of second-year students.

Paul's story

First year

My first year . . . The big thing that I noticed is that in sixth form, you know, we would talk, you know . . . 'I think this' and 'I think that' . . . In university, it is completely different: I didn't say anything in lectures and that was something that I struggled with. But closer to the second semester, I kind of grasped it and managed to complete my assignments all right.

I think overall my first year went quite well. I got 64 per cent or something at the end of the first year which meant I was on for a 2:1. So I was happy with that, yeah. I had a very helpful personal tutor in the first year, but she retired at the end of the first year. We didn't get assigned a new one, so I think that probably changed things . . .

Effort-wise, I thought, it was quite low. And some of the modules didn't seem relevant (now, reflecting back, I understand that they actually were quite useful). There was a lot of free time that let me do things – I started getting into athletics and taking the gym more seriously. The more time you have the less you seem to get done, you know, but I can see why you have a lot of free time because, you know, students who are not from Liverpool – they are going to need time to know what is around and stuff. We locals know everything and have been everywhere.

In summer, I went on a lads' holiday with my friends from home. With regard to uni in summer, not much got done if I'm honest. I just thought – right, I got that mark, I put all the books to one side and thought I have got, I don't know, 10 weeks to just chill. Oh, yeah, I worked in a café – it kept me through summer. I was looking forward to going back to uni; there is only so much time that you can spend doing nothing, but the buzz of going to university had definitely ended.

Second year

In the second year, the reality started to kick in, it's not going to be as easy, and they make you aware in your first year you only needed 40 per cent to pass, but in second year, it was 25 per cent of my final mark. So you start to think, OK, these marks count, I need to start getting a fair reflection of what is going into that.

I think we picked two optional modules in second year, and there were a lot of core modules. I didn't really know if it was enough or not enough because I didn't really know at that stage what it was I wanted to do within [my subject]. I looked through the Blackboard folder to see what optional modules were available. Some of them were so broad, which I guess was good because I didn't know what I wanted to do. But if I did know, then I would have wanted the information to be more specific.

As to the social side . . . In the first year, I spent a lot of time with a girl I knew from school (she was also on my course). I didn't sort of interact with the other students as much, which in the second year became quite an issue because she dropped out at the end of the first year, so I was sort of left isolated in a way.

Because my course was a sandwich course, you were meant to do a placement in the third year. There was a big, big push on prepping yourself: look for the placements, get your CV good. We would have a module preparing us for placements. We did it and then the careers centre would now and then send emails and say – oh, you know, 'how are you getting on?' But a real good thing that they did once a week, maybe twice a week, they would send you a big long list with all the vacancies – a list of all the vacancies, running from vacancies that end in a week to vacancies that end in two or three months . . . Yeah, but in the first semester, I didn't really bat an eyelid, I just thought . . . I don't know . . . I wasn't busy.

In the first semester . . . it was just mainly the placement stuff. I think the teacher just expected you to get on with that. I didn't use my time as efficiently as probably I should have done, yeah, so with the work I didn't really make any advancement until the second semester, to be honest. I just sort of got what I needed to get done in the first semester and then, you know, at Christmas it goes really quick, it's there before you know it . . . And I guess the main thing I was thinking of was just to get through this first semester, and my attendance in second year was especially poor, I remember I had a few talks about my attendance. Instead of attending lectures, I was often going to the gym or socialising with friends. I guess just doing things that I wanted to do but probably shouldn't have been doing. It was similar to quite a few people, certainly my friends in uni – they all seemed to take a back seat in the second year. Definitely . . . we would spend more time just talking; instead of going to the library to do work, we would go to the library and play our games, or whatever . . .

And then Christmas came, and we came back from Christmas. I started to think: wow, I need to get a placement before this summer and that sort of went . . . And my attention turned from assessments to placements, which meant that the modules that I was interested in – they took priority along with the placement, but the ones that I wasn't interested in I basically neglected.

I failed one module because I just really didn't like it. Took a back seat and failed another one as well, but they are modules that I shouldn't have failed and if I had applied myself better to them I could have passed them, definitely. Because your attention was in a sense just sort of split between trying to find a placement and keep going. There was a bit of laziness in there, I suppose, as well the fact that the end of university is still far away. I had to re-sit my exam in the summer, but I got a compensatory fail for one but I had to re-sit another.

The second semester was definitely better because failing the module in the first semester sort of gave me a bit of a kick to say: you are slacking too much here, and then there was obviously getting on with preparation for work.

Yes, that just shows how little I was interacting with it, but then realising I had failed definitely give me a kick and I started putting more effort in, because I was looking for placements. A lot of the emphasis in the second semester was definitely on placements, you know, even modules that weren't related to place-ments. Lecturers would spend the first 10 minutes asking 'how is everybody get-ting on with their placements?' At some point, I just got sick of hearing about placements.

I started to apply for placements more actively in the second semester. I started with sort of 'ideal' jobs, rather than practical ones that I was more likely to get. But then in the second semester, a lot more variety came up. In my head, I wanted to stay locally, I don't know the reason for that. I stayed at home for uni because I did that right at the last minute and I didn't want to get rubbish halls, so I just thought it's close, so I will stay at home. I guess money was an incen-tive, you would save more money. Later I started applying for placements in the North, I think North West or a different country was what I wanted. I didn't want to stay in this country and move to London or something. I didn't get a placement in the end and went straight into the third year.

My struggle with getting a placement had a knock on effect on my atti-tude towards uni. I was starting to feel more negative towards it. I guess as well seeing the bad marks that made me quite anxious, I had even thought of dropping out. I did let work drift, especially in the first year. During assess-ment time, my room was spotless everyday because I would tidy my room instead of doing work.

Later, in the second year, I got a desk, started to buy books and get books from the library, and I think the whole workplace just started to look more like a university student's workspace. I think it was just a mental thing that changed: when I got my workspace sorted at home, I started taking my studies more seri-ously. I was more engaged with the studies definitely in the second semester than the first semester which I think is mainly due to failing modules in the first semes-ter, but I am glad I had done that because I might not have stepped up the work.

In terms of marks . . . They were indeed lower . . . Yes, first year I got mid- to low 60s and second year because I failed I think it was three modules: yeah, I got 51 per cent which is obviously a good 10 per cent drop.

Going into the third year made me think that I've got some real work to do here because I was determined not to leave uni with less than a 2:1. Because I know you look at jobs and stuff, especially if I am aspiring for those jobs, you have got to have a 2:1.

After the second year, in summer, again, I was just really going out and doing what 19- and 20-year-olds do, yeah, but I think the fact that I did so little over the summer for such a long period of time had made it hard to get back into uni, to come back for the third year. And the marks in second year . . . you are definitely more conscious of them, you work out in your head: what do I need to get in the third year? I would do it so many times throughout the year, I would get one mark wrong and make the calculation again – which was a good thing looking back, because it kept me thinking, wow, I really can't relax here.

Third year

The third year was different. I was so engaged all the time. Because the modules were what I wanted to do, and even the core modules I found really interesting, that made me do more reading outside, and even just after the lectures or something I would go to the library, spend 20 minutes, get a book out, get the notes, make some more notes, and that definitely would help me, because towards exam time it was a lot more fresh.

The interaction with students was a hard part . . . They were the year above and with me not being in that year there was no one in my group that I recognised from the year before. We had a group work project. We were told to choose groups, but I was sort of left isolated a bit. Because I didn't know many people I was left with two people, two international students, and one girl who was quite quiet. It was quite interesting, but also that let me take quite a natural leadership role which I like. Being leader, I definitely developed skills, you know, confidence and initiative.

In the final year, my approach to work completely changed. I actually got the work done and then you have got time to, you know, to do the other things instead of doing things and then looking at uni work at the last minute. And that then also made me do first drafts and because I had the work done for the deadline I could then give it to my mum to do a proof read or something . . . That had a knock-on effect on the marks. In fact, I actually handed a piece of coursework in a week early, which was unheard of for me. I think as well in the final year you start to see the relevance of what you are doing and how that will affect you after university and you start to get more of a sense that if you don't get the grade it's you that misses out, not the teacher, so you start thinking, wow, yeah, you need to put the work in and get the grades.

Reflecting back on the whole experience

I think students need to be more aware of why they do things, like preparation for placement – as far as I was concerned, this was just brushing up the CV and, you know, not making me more employable but making me look more employable. I remember we got told to keep a journal at an earlier stage, I said no, I am not doing that, but I think that is because of a lack of understanding of why.

I think that being more proactive and having regular meetings with a personal tutor or another member of staff would have made all the difference to me. Probably because my personal tutor had gone, nobody told me 'look, you are failing, the marks are really not up to scratch'. I could have turned that around in the second half of the second year. I think the big motivator for people each year is the marks, you know . . .

This vignette is edited from the transcript of an interview with Paul (a pseudonym). He ended up with a 2:1 (an upper second-class honours degree).

Chapter 1

Why study the second year?

Mantz Yorke

Paul is not unique

Most teachers will come across quite a few Pauls (or Paulas) during their careers, even though they may not be privy to the kinds of experiences – such as the lack of focus, the drift, the seductiveness of socialising, the difficulties with relationships and the limited commitment to second-year work – that are recounted in the vignette at the start of this book. It is not uncommon to find study programmes in which students' marks dip in the second year: some of the dipping may be attributable to the psychological dimension of students' experiences, some may be more broadly sociological in character and some may reflect characteristics of the programme of study and institution. Whatever the causes of a second-year dip (and they are often complex), a concern for student success indicates that institutions could with advantage investigate the second-year experience, whether or not students' marks show a dip.

'Second-year blues' in the United Kingdom

The literature provides some evidence to support the more anecdotal evidence of a dip in second-year grades. Lieberman and Remedios (2007) found, in relation to four-year degree programmes at a Scottish university, that there were drops in students' ratings of their interest in their subject of study, their enjoyment and their orientation towards mastery from the first year – drops that never recovered in the subsequent years. Jacobs and Newstead (2000) had previously conducted, in an English university, two studies of psychology students' motivation towards aspects of their subject. They found a decline in the students' perceptions of the importance of both subject-specific and generic skills over the first two years of the degree programme, but a recovery in the final year. Aspects of broader experience (ranging from meeting with professional psychologists to having a good social life and developing as a person) exhibited a similar pattern. Jacobs and Newstead (2000: 252) observed that their findings

> may constitute empirical evidence for what is sometimes called 'second year blues'. Students maintain their interest in skills and experiences (and

some aspects of knowledge) over the first year of their studies but then lose motivation in the second year. The encouraging message is that motivation in many areas recovers in the final year.

In 2007, it was noticed at Liverpool John Moores University that only around 45 per cent of graduates achieved a 'good honours degree' (first-class or upper-second-class honours at bachelor's level), whereas in similar institutions, the percentage was higher. The question prompted an examination of student record data in order to determine whether these might offer some clues. An initial analysis of some 7,000 module results from students graduating in 2008 revealed that undergraduate student performance on 24-credit modules across the institution had dipped in the second year of study. In their second year, only 32 per cent of students had achieved grades that could be categorised as being compatible with the level of a 'good honours degree', compared to 36 per cent in their first year and 46 per cent in their third and final years. Could this apparent 'second-year dip' be prejudicing final-year success?

Subsequent analyses of the mean marks achieved by student cohorts in each academic year showed that in a number of the university's programmes of study there was a dip in performance in the second year (of typically three), followed in almost all of these cases by a rise in the final year, whereas in others, there was a progressive rise in mean mark (Figure 1.1). The most obvious question was why apparent dips in students' second-year performance might be arising.

These findings, which are a reasonable fit with those in the literature, prompted the range of investigations set out in the chapters of this book.

The 'sophomore slump' in the United States

In the United States, the dip in second-year performance has been termed the 'sophomore slump'[1] and has been the focus of study over a considerable period of time (e.g. Freedman, 1956; Furr and Gannoway, 1982; Pattengale and Schreiner, 2000; Graunke and Woosley, 2005; Gump, 2007), though studies have tended to be sporadic rather than systematic, which is a justification for the call by Hunter et al. (2010: 29) for institutions to research their sophomores. Paralleling findings by Jacobs and Newstead (2000), Pattengale and Schreiner (2000: vi) observed that many second-year students 'suffer from reduced motivation or apathy, declining grade point averages, or a letdown from their first year'. Graunke and Woosley (2005) pointed to the possible influence of a lack of direction and a sense of disconnection in second-year students. More recently, the higher education consultants Noel-Levitz (2013) reported that only three-quarters of second-year students at four-year private and public institutions were able to affirm that they 'felt energized' by the ideas they were learning in most of their classes and that only two-thirds of second-year students at two-year public institutions were able to affirm the statement 'I have many friends and feel at home here'. The downside of these findings is

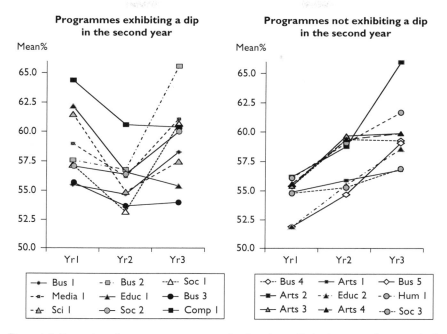

Programmes exhibiting a dip in the second year

Mean%

Programmes not exhibiting a dip in the second year

Mean%

—◆— Bus 1	- ◻· Bus 2	··△·· Soc 1		-◇-- Bus 4	—■— Arts 1	-◇— Bus 5
- ◆- Media 1	—▲— Educ 1	—●— Bus 3		—■— Arts 2	-▲· Educ 2	-●· Hum 1
-△- Sci 1	—⊙— Soc 2	—■— Comp 1		—▲— Arts 3	—▲— Arts 4	-●-- Soc 3

Figure 1.1 Examples of programme mean marks showing a dip in the second year and of programme means showing no such dip

Notes
Bus = business-related programme; Soc = social science; Educ = education; Sci = science-based;
Comp = computing-based; Media and Arts are self-explanatory.

that a non-trivial minority of second-year students were having an experience in higher education that was less than ideal.

It has been recognised in the USA that second-year students have substantial needs but receive the least attention of all undergraduates (Pattengale and Schreiner, 2000; Graunke and Woosley, 2005; Gahagan and Hunter, 2006), leading some to refer to the second year as the 'forgotten year' (Tobolowsky, 2008; Hunter *et al.*, 2010).

The second-year slump: possible causes

Undertaking study in higher education is a demanding and complex process. A consequence of this is that, where students' second-year performance is less than optimal (and may represent a falling-back from the level achieved during the first year), identifying causes is often not straightforward – there are simply too many variables at play.

Three broad areas of 'the student experience' subsume possible influences on the 'sophomore slump' (where it is observed, and – less easy to detect – where second-year performance appears to have risen but, in fact, has risen less than it might have done, given other circumstances):

- the psychological make-up of the student, including goal orientation and subject desire (Lieberman and Remedios, 2007), commitment (Graunke and Woosley, 2005; Schaller, 2005; Sheard and Golby, 2007) and self-competency beliefs (Bruinsma, 2004);
- curriculum-related matters, including programme design and pedagogy, differences in marking criteria and grading (Yorke, 2008) and a mismatch between staff and student expectations of learning outcomes (Maclellan, 2001); and
- the influence of extraneous factors such as the need to undertake part-time work while studying, and to sort out accommodation issues and adventitious events.

For many students, the causes of underperformance are interrelated: for example, the weakly motivated student may have their motivation influenced by the pedagogy of the programme and/or the need to undertake part-time employment to provide the financial support needed to sustain their studies. One cause does not fit all.

There is often a reaction to the 'high' of an initial engagement. Writers and recording stars often find difficulty in sustaining an initial success – the 'second novel syndrome' or 'second album syndrome'. Promoted football teams quite often survive in the higher league during their first season but are relegated the season afterwards, as the records of the English Premier League testify. A government elected to popular acclaim can find that the enthusiasm fades away – as opinion polls and mid-term elections frequently demonstrate – and the adrenalin burst of the next election is a long way from kicking in.

For students new to higher education, there is often a heady mixture of novelty, excitement and apprehension to provide a charge to the first year, which may not reappear until the final year when the end of the programme approaches, a substantial piece of individually relevant work (such as a project or dissertation) has to be completed and the next transition – usually into employment – has to be negotiated. With the first year being a period of transition and the final year still somewhat distant, some students may find the second year a particularly good opportunity for distraction and spend more time in non-academic aspects of higher education such as sports, participating in societies and having a good time socially. In contrast, others may see their second year as being 'where the serious work begins' (a perception possibly assisted by the fact that students have a greater opportunity to choose some of their modules, with perhaps an eye to their future beyond higher education).

Analyses of qualitative data from analogues of the National Student Survey completed at Liverpool John Moores University (presented in Chapter 3) suggest that students' perceptions of various aspects of their experience tend to undergo a shift between the first and second years. Furthermore, there are hints from empirical evidence that the issues that students bring to the institutional counselling service may be rather different in the second year from those presented in the first year. More broadly, the level of personal tutor support may be lower in the second year. The point at issue here is that students' focus in respect of study in higher education is not necessarily consistent throughout a programme of study, which may have implications for engagement and success.

Students enter higher education for a variety of reasons, and not necessarily because they have a strong desire to advance their knowledge of a particular subject. Some have entered higher education in the United Kingdom because of expectations laid upon them by family and/or school, and may not yet have formed a clear view of what they wanted to achieve in life. In the United States, a generalist first two years may result in second-year students being in a state of uncertainty about their choice of major. A few find that the subject they thought they would find interesting turns out not to be as expected: a naive projection of school success or of a highly involving hobby can lead to disillusionment.

Sometimes, the first year is viewed by the institution as an extended period of induction. This can be for praiseworthy reasons such as giving students who are disadvantaged by a lack of family background and other causes sufficient time to adjust to the expectations of higher education. On the other hand, such an easing-in can become a too-easy experience, leading students towards an unjustified evaluation of their achievements and a rosier perspective on their subsequent years of study than is warranted – not least because they may not have developed adequately their capacity for independent study. (There is a risk for institutions here, in that they may be merely deferring potential problems regarding retention.)

In England, Wales and Northern Ireland,[2] it is typically the case that a student's honours degree classification is determined by performances in the final two of the three years of academic study (where a placement year is incorporated into a four-year programme – normally in the third year – the results from the placement year do not carry much weight in the classification). It is from the second year on that students are expected to work at honours level,[3] and this can be a shock if the first year has been a relatively comfortable experience, academically. It should be noted at this point that students who have studied a subject at A-level may find themselves repeating material in the early stages of their degree programme: possible consequences are boredom, taking study too lightly, overconfidence and subsequent difficulty in getting to terms with a step-change in academic demand in the second year. Mature students, too, may find the first year does not stretch them as much as they had expected.

Particular attention is often given to the first and final years of a programme (for understandable educational reasons). A question that arises is whether the second year is given a definite character, or whether it is seen as simply lying between the first and final years, and not in need of further induction activity.[4] One might look for the answer in terms of the learning outcomes specified for the components of the study programme as a whole in order to determine whether those set for the second year are distinctive. However, the difficulty with this is that the same kinds of wording are used at different levels, with the difference lying in the ways in which apparently common language is interpreted in practice. Analyses of curricula, therefore, need to dig below the veneer of what can often be a rather standardised – indeed, bureaucratic – terminology of formal specifications. A different line of inquiry, suggested from time to time by academics, is that some curricular components that are needed as base-material for final-year study are 'bunched' in second-year curricula. The problem from the students' perspective is that they might not, at that time, perceive the relevance of these components and/or perceive them as 'too difficult' (perhaps prompting self-doubt, especially if they are still coming to terms with the demands of independent study) and hence lack some motivation to put the necessary effort in.

Many students find the need to undertake part-time employment in order to support themselves through their programmes of study. Evidence from the United States indicates that this can actually be advantageous if undertaken on campus, but disadvantageous if off campus (Pascarella and Terenzini, 2005): the extension of the relationship between student and institution seems to be of key importance. Students in the United Kingdom who are disadvantaged in various ways (e.g. by being relatively poor financially or who have responsibilities for dependants) may spend disproportionate amounts of time on earning in order to give themselves a bit more scope to study in their final year (when their marks typically receive a higher weighting than those awarded in the second year). Part-time employment can affect attendance in respect of both the formal and informal aspects of higher education. Attendance can also be affected by the outcome of students' calculations as to whether it is necessary for them to attend scheduled teaching sessions if they have decided on the work they intend to do in order to satisfy the assessment requirements for a module.

Finally, there are always unpredictable events which affect individual students (such as accidents, health-related issues, dealing with accommodation difficulties), though it is doubtful whether these can be tied disproportionately to the second-year experience.

Given that so many variables can be in play, and can operate with varying salience across cohorts of students, it is not surprising that Graunke and Woosley (2005) wrote that evidence regarding causes of the 'sophomore slump' was inconclusive. Consequently, any hunt for the cause of decrements in second-year performance is unlikely to be productive. What can be done, however, is to look at the issue probabilistically, in both quantitative and qualitative terms, in order to gain a richer appreciation of what influences the second-year performance and hence where it might be enhanced (whether or not a 'slump' might be observed). This necessitates a multi-dimensional exploration of 'the second-year experience'. This exploration can include various kinds of inquiry of students as to the nature of their experience, the gathering of perceptions from academic and support staff and the mining of potentially rich seams of data from what in contemporary higher education institutions is a plethora of datasets (some being necessary to satisfy administrative and/or external requirements, while others may constitute the internal records of a particular institutional component). Some issues are institution-wide, some are best addressed at departmental (or other organisational unit) level and others may be most appropriately pursued by individuals: 'who should do what' and how the various pieces of a rather complex analytical jigsaw are put together are structural issues that need to be addressed.

Researching the institution

Institutions routinely collect huge amounts of data about students and their performance, not to mention data relating to other aspects of institutional functioning. 'Institutional research', as a component of institutional functioning, is well established in the United States and has developed in Europe, Australia and elsewhere in the world. However, analyses such as those that have identified the 'sophomore slump' are more common in the USA than in the United Kingdom (Tight, 2007): a study by Yorke *et al.* (2005) had earlier pointed out that institutions could make more of the potential inherent in the datasets that they assemble.

Volkwein (1999) characterised institutional research as a matrix of four broad areas, admitting that the boundaries between them were fuzzy (the main box in Figure 1.2). Institutional researchers may:

A   collect and present data for the institution's internal administrative purposes,
B   use existing or freshly gathered data to inform the development of professional practices,
C   collect and present data for external audiences (presentation possibly including an element of 'spin'), and
D   undertake studies with a level of rigour appropriate to peer-reviewed educational research.

Subsequently, Serban (2002) added a fifth area of activity, knowledge management, which Volkwein (2008) built into a later formulation. However, knowledge management may or may not be undertaken by an institutional researcher, since much depends on the role and status of such personnel. It may more usefully be seen as the process by which the institutional (and its sub-institutional) components develop and implement policy. However one construes knowledge management, it chimes with contemporary expectations that policy and practice will be evidence informed (e.g. Higher Education Academy [HEA], 2008; Strick and Creagh, 2008; Bond, 2009).

This book takes as its focus Volkwein's area B, the enhancement of provision through the use of quantitative and qualitative research. The focus widens into area A because of the managerial and administrative implications of dealing with the outcomes of research, and perhaps also into area C, in that

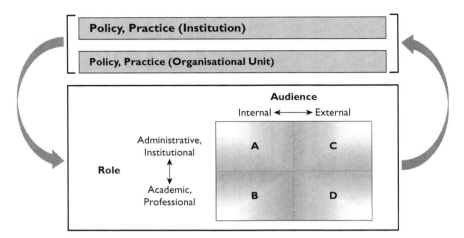

Figure 1.2 An adaptation of Volkwein's matrix, showing the relationship between institutional research and policy

institutions – especially in a competitive market for students – may wish to use the outcomes of institutional research for promotional purposes. The primary purpose, institutional benefit, may necessitate the use of data that were collected by the institution for a different purpose and, as a consequence, may not be ideal but may be merely 'good enough' for the purpose at hand.[5]

The policy context

The second-year experience, as part of the totality of a student's engagement with higher education, needs to be set in the broader context of state and institutional policy. Student success, provided it is not bought at the expense of lowered academic standards, is self-evidently a desirable outcome, not least because governments around the world stress the importance of their higher education systems for national prosperity. Successful completion of programmes of study in higher education provides the flow of graduates that is necessary to support economic development, with 'graduate attributes' and 'employability' being seen as markers of the practical value of graduates in the labour market. For the individual graduate, the value of their qualification is typically indexed in financial terms. Blundell *et al.* (2000) showed that not completing one's programme was financially disadvantageous for men (but not for women) in the United Kingdom. More recently, Purcell *et al.* (2012) have shown a similar result based on students (irrespective of gender) who applied to enter higher education in 2006 and who had subsequently gained employment.[6] Furthermore, Purcell *et al.* indicate that the salary premium attached to graduate status has declined in the United Kingdom over a considerable period of years. However, the focus on financial return distracts from other important benefits that accrue from engagement in higher education, such as those in the areas of health and general quality of life (see, for example, Institute for Higher Education Policy [IHEP], 1998; Bynner and Egerton, 2001; Bynner *et al.*, 2003; Pascarella and Terenzini, 2005; Murray, 2009; Brennan *et al.*, 2013).

Students who do not complete programmes of study are often associated with pejorative terms such as 'dropout' and 'wastage', when a more nuanced perspective is desirable. There are cultural differences regarding part-completion of a programme of study: Weko (2004) noted that, in the United States, value was placed on the credits that students had actually achieved,[7] whereas in the United Kingdom part-completion of a programme tended to be viewed in terms of students not having achieved the award being sought.

The issue of student retention has been a focus of higher education policy in the United States, Australia and the United Kingdom, among other countries, since at state[8] level there are implications for both public finances (though the public finance element varies markedly between different higher education systems) and for quality assurance (where the state seeks to assure students that higher education provision is of at least satisfactory quality). Concerns over the extent to which students do not complete their programmes of study can lead to queries as to whether non-completion might be related to the quality of the higher education experience although the modelling of retention and early departure (e.g. Tinto, 1993; Bean and Eaton, 2000; Yorke and Longden, 2004) and a host of empirical studies have shown that non-completion typically involves a congeries of interlocking influences. In the United Kingdom, developments in higher education policy led to calls to revisit issues of student success (Longden, 2002; Haggis, 2006; McQueen, 2009). McQueen (2009) argued that issues may be less to do with social integration but more with increasing disaffection arising from a mismatch between the 'Success for All' education promoted by the United Kingdom Government's policy (Department for Education and Skills, 2002) and the reality of the contemporary undergraduate experience where institutions are challenged to meet the needs of an increasingly diverse student population.

Retention self-evidently has significant implications for both institutions and students. For institutions, non-completion translates into lost income, with contingencies possibly including programme closure and loss of reputation and – at the extreme – a declining spiral of enrolment. For students, the benefit of part-completion has to be set against the costs of earnings foregone and earnings potentially unrealised. Avoiding the demoralisation of an apparent decline in second-year performance may for some students make the difference between premature departure from the institution and successful completion of the programme.

Beginnings and endings as foci of attention

The first-year student experience is, for many students, a critical determinant of whether they persist in, or depart from, higher education. The dominant reasons given by students who withdrew during, or at the end of, their first year in the United Kingdom were: having made the wrong choice of programme, academic difficulties, financial problems and three kinds of dissatisfaction – with the student experience, with institutional provision and with the environment in which the institution was situated (Yorke, 1999). These findings were echoed by Davies and Elias (2003). A broadly similar pattern of reasons for non-continuation was again found by Yorke and Longden (2008). These studies involved students who, in the main, were following three-year programmes whose curricular content was established from the beginning. Where a four-year programme can be characterised as '2 + 2', with students opting for majors having pursued a general programme in the first two years, the end of the second year can become a point of departure because the 'break' offers a convenient point at which students can reorient or abandon their studies with minimum disruptiveness.

The importance of the first-year experience is emphasised by the attention given to it in surveys, examples being Ruiz et al. (2010) in the United States, James et al. (2009) in Australia and Yorke and Longden (2007) in the United Kingdom. The realisation that the first year of study can be particularly challenging is now widespread internationally, with various initiatives being undertaken to make the early stages of a programme in higher education a less formidable transition. For example, 'first-year seminars' have been widely adopted in the United States as vehicles for easing the transition into higher education where the educational approach can be very different from the incoming students' previous educational experience. Also, the first-year experience has figured prominently in academic conferences, such as those run annually by the National Resource Center for The First-Year Experience and Students in Transition at the University of South Carolina,[9] and by Queensland University of Technology[10] and, in Europe, as the rationale for events organised under the banner of the European First Year Experience.[11]

The 'other end' of the undergraduate experience is also acknowledged as being important, since it is the point at which full-time students leave higher education, typically for employment. The primary focus of attention is on graduate outcomes (in terms of summative assessments of academic achievements and – less formalised – 'generic' capabilities that are highly valued in the labour market). Students are asked about their experiences of higher education programmes: in Australia, this has been undertaken shortly after graduation since 1993, using the Course Experience Questionnaire (which has evolved from its original form over the years); in the United Kingdom, the National Student Survey of final-year students has been in place since 2005. Both instruments ask, albeit in a very limited way, about the development of 'generic' capabilities relevant to workplaces and wider society.[12] These instruments are taken seriously by institutions, despite their methodological weaknesses, since they end up in one form or another in 'league tables' or rankings and have the potential to influence applications for places.

There is unevenness in the attention given to the stages of the 'student life cycle'. Although there have been a number of depictions of this life cycle as a closed circle, it is better represented as an expanding spiral (Figure 1.3) in order to emphasise the importance of any programme of study for expanding horizons and capabilities,[13] and its potential to lead into further cycles of formal and informal study.

Improving students' experience of the middle years

There are signs that the middle years of the student experience are beginning to be afforded greater attention: in the United States, for example,

- Sanchez-Leguelinel (2008) wrote of the value of peer initiatives in enhancing the retention of sophomores;
- Winona State University has instituted a 'Sophomore Business Bridge Program' for its College of Business, with the intention that the 'real-life' experience will assist retention;[14]
- Valdosta State University embarked on a Sophomore Year Experience Plan (Peguesse, 2008);
- Minnesota State University Mankato has created web-pages designed to help sophomores deal with the issue of 'sophomore slump';[15]
- The University of North Carolina at Charlotte has run surveys of sophomores;[16] and
- The University of Denver compiled a pamphlet offering guidance for parents of sophomores.[17]

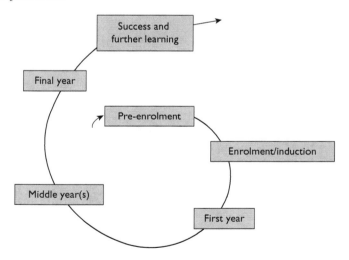

Figure 1.3 The student life-spiral, representing an undergraduate programme

Notes
Some models of the student life cycle emphasise the raising of aspirations, especially among disadvantaged school pupils, as a necessary condition for getting to the pre-enrolment stage.

Following earlier publications from the National Resource Center for The First-Year Experience and Students in Transition (Pattengale and Schreiner, 2000; Tobolowsky and Cox, 2007), a strong encouragement to focus on the sophomore year has been provided by Hunter *et al.* (2010) in their book *Helping Sophomores Succeed: Understanding and Improving the Second-Year Experience*. This book is a very helpful compendium of knowledge and experience based on programmes in the United States, covering the background literature, a range of interventions whose purpose is to enhance the engagement of second-year students and how institutions as a whole might respond to the challenge of optimising the second-year experience. A list of 35 institutions that run programmes in support of sophomores can be found on the Center's website.[18] An example of how an institution is responding to 'the sophomore challenge' is given by Fisher *et al.* (2011) who presented to their accreditation agency (the Southern Association of Colleges and Schools) proposals for the enhancement of the quality of sophomore education at Belmont University that were well grounded in the literature (and strongly influenced by Hunter *et al.*, 2010).

Elsewhere,

- Students in the field of building and civil engineering at Victoria University of Technology in Australia were markedly less enthused by their second-year studies, seeing them as very theoretical and without strong connection to practice (Evans *et al.*, 1999). The university took steps to increase the practical element of the second-year curriculum.
- Richardson (2004) reported from a post-92 university in the UK that students had a 'false sense of security' after their first year and that the workload of the second year was markedly more demanding.
- Scott and Cashmore (2012) describe a video-diary study involving second-year students of biosciences at Leicester University, which pointed to the challenges of heavier workloads and of moving from halls of residence into 'student houses'.
- At the University of Huddersfield, a project has been started that focuses on overcoming 'second-year blues' through innovations aiming to support the development of students' learning at 'intermediate level'.[19]
- Deakin University in Australia noted a slump in the grades of second-year students completing science courses and has worked since 2009 to counter this.[20]

Signals and noise

It is already apparent that the second-year experience (as are the experiences on either side) is shot through with complexity which includes influences at a variety of levels ranging from the personal to the institutional, and even at times extending to influences impacting on institutions. The chapters that follow seek to identify signals among this 'noise' that can help readers (in whatever institutional position they hold) to identify issues that impact on the experiences of second-year students and to develop, where it is open to them to do so, ways of mitigating problems.

Notes

1 The term is often attributed to Freedman (1956): however, it seems to have pre-dated his article since his study found no evidence for such a (named) slump at Vassar College.
2 The typical structure of honours degrees in Scotland and Australia is '3 + 1', with the final year being devoted to study at honours level.
3 Most institutions differentiate the second and third years in 'Part 2' of the hon-ours degree programme, but a few have an undifferentiated Part 2 structure.
4 Students transferring into a programme at the beginning of the second year are particularly likely to be disadvantaged if there is no induction activity.
5 A caution always has to be entered in respect of institutional data, since they may be less than perfect because of the problems with data entry or changes in the way that externally collected data are handled. Yorke (2011) provides some examples.
6 A few 'non-completers' performed as well as graduates at the top-end of the salary scale. No explanation is given, but it might be speculated that these were people who left higher education because their expertise, rather than a formal qualifica-tion, was deemed by employers to be of high value to them.
7 Robertson (2002, para 194ff) had earlier shown that, in the United States, the return on a student's investment in higher education correlated positively with the amount of higher education completed.
8 The word 'state' here does not differentiate between a nation-state (e.g. England, Republic of Ireland) and individual states within a federal nation, as is the case in Australia and the United States. The differentiation is of limited significance for intra-institutional matters and is not pursued in this book.
9 See http://www.sc.edu/fye/.
10 See http://www.fyhe.qut.edu.au/.
11 See http://www.efye.eu/.
12 Section 17 of the 2013 version of the National Survey of Student Engagement (NSSE) used in the United States (see http://nsse.iub.edu/pdf/survey_instru-ments/2013/2013%20NSSE%20Instrument.pdf) also asks students about their development of 'generic' capabilities, though this is used during their programmes of study: the Student Engagement Questionnaire, one of three instruments in the Australasian Survey of Student Engagement (AUSSE) (see http://www.acer.edu.au/files/AUSSE_2011_SEQ.pdf) has a similar set of questions.
13 The 'life-spiral' embodies both the refining of an existing cognitive scheme through the assimilation of new information and the scheme's development in order to accommodate information that does not fit it. Piaget (1929/2000), writ-ing of child development, referred to assimilation and accommodation, as in the wider human context does Kelly (1955) when he refers to the definition and extension of a person's construct system.
14 See https://www.winona.edu/career/Business-Bridge.asp.
15 See http://www.mnsu.edu/students/sophomores/.
16 See https://ir.uncc.edu/survey-results/sophomore.
17 This is no longer available electronically.
18 Navigated from http://www.sc.edu/fye/resources/soph/index.html.
19 See http://www.hud.ac.uk/tali/projects/tl_projects_13/second%20year%20blues/.
20 See an abstract at http://ojs-prod.library.usyd.edu.au/index.php/IISME/article/viewFile/4832/5522.

Chapter 2

Defining the second year

Clare Milsom and Mantz Yorke

Finding the second-year focus

This chapter explores the academic characteristics that define the second year. We argue that the second year is left relatively undefined as, in a three-year undergraduate degree programme, it is sandwiched between the first and final years, both of which are more commonly understood. The divergent attention on the beginning and end of programmes has implications for the quality of the programme as a whole. If the second year of a three-year full-time programme lacks a clear focus, then teaching, learning and student achievement may be adversely affected. Providing a positive academic identity for the second-year experience is paramount. Most academic frameworks seem to imply a linear acquisition of level-specific learning outcomes. The concept of the 'spiral curriculum' (Bruner, 1960), mentioned in Chapter 1, provides an alternative view that implies that even the most complex objectives can be achieved at the appropriate level in the first year through frequent reinforcement and application. Static outcome-based frameworks and models may be taken to present an over-simplified understanding of the characteristics of each level of learning in an academic programme. Quality frameworks and level descriptors attempt to ascribe sets of unique characteristics to each year in a programme of study. These characteristics position the second year as an intermediate experience between two more strongly articulated years.

Factors influencing the second-year experience

The second year of a three-year undergraduate programme in higher education can be problematic for teachers and students due to a number of factors. These factors also apply, *mutatis mutandis*, to programmes of other durations, for example, in the US and Scotland where the third and fourth years are more clearly defined by the students' academic specialism. Converging influences make the definition of the second year elusive for a number of reasons:

1   Academic standards on entry to, and at the exit from, a university academic programme are clearly defined. There are, of course, variations on the entry side such as differing entry requirements, with some students enrolling largely on the basis of life-experience rather than formal qualifications. There is also variation

on the exit side as different university programmes emphasise different kinds of achievements, for example, the primarily vocational as opposed to the primarily academic. However, the relatively firm anchor-points at the beginning and end are less well complemented in the middle of the programme despite the existence of qualifications frameworks, as will be discussed later in the chapter.

2   Undergraduate programmes aim to develop autonomous learners who are intellectually self-reliant, able to appraise material critically and to exercise well-grounded judgement in response to the situations they face. For many, and particularly for entrants direct from school, the undergraduate experience is a journey from acquiescence, relying on 'authority figures' (in particular, teachers), to the autonomy of self-determination and self-regulation. A number of writers on student development have, from their varied positions and with differing use of terminology, pointed to this trajectory (see, for example, Kohlberg, 1964; King and Kitchener, 1994; Perry, 1998; Kuhn and Weinstock, 2002; and Baxter Magolda, 2009). Baxter Magolda (2009, p. 144) puts the position thus:

> Guiding learners through the transformation from authority dependence to self-authorship is a primary challenge for twenty-first century higher education.

3   Furthermore, students adapt to the academic demands that higher education is making on them at different rates. In the vernacular, some may not 'get it' until well into their first year (Leckey and Cook, 1999) – and, for some, later still. What may have worked well for them at school, such as using frequent feedback on pieces of work to produce an authority-approved 'answer' to a set task, may prove less successful where they are expected to work with a high amount of autonomy and independence.[1] Students often need support – and time – to come to terms with the expectations of higher education (see, for example, Fazey and Fazey, 2001; Leathwood and O'Connell, 2003; Pokorny and Pokorny, 2005). Booth (2005, p. 2) emphasises the importance of autonomy in history programmes:

> [N]ew undergraduates often see the tutor as the 'expert' who can (and perhaps should) give them 'the information'. By contrast university history teachers emphasise the need for student autonomy and independent judgement.

4   The second year may be particularly challenging for students who studied their chosen academic discipline at an advanced level in school. These students may have coasted comfortably during their first year, drawing on what they had already learned and using their previous study strategies, without much adjustment to the demands of higher education. Students who are giving the academic discipline prominence for the first time in their studies will have had to face a new or newish subject while adjusting to the demands of higher education. Having had to adapt their learning approaches, those new

to the academic discipline might find themselves better placed to cope with the second year's studies.

5   Differentiating levels of study is far from straightforward. A case can be made for pupils and students operating according to all six of the levels in Bloom's (1956) *Taxonomy of Educational Objectives* (or its more recent formulation in Anderson and Krathwohl, 2001).[2] The higher one goes in education, the difference is the greater inclusivity of the subject content: Box 2.1 illustrates something of the point. The 'spiral curriculum' (Bruner, 1960), mentioned in Chapter 1, suggests that simplistic notions of 'level' are inadequate to cope with curricular complexity. In some curricula, though, the second year's studies are well defined. The problem for some students may be that they find the subject material hard: they may be required to engage with subject material with which they have little or no prior experience – for instance, being faced with a research methodology module as a precursor to some form of final-year project. There might also be a heavy academic demand as the intellectual decks are being cleared in preparation for the final year. The outcome might in either case be some decrement (in mark terms) relative to

---

Box 2.1   One person's experience of 'levels' in educational curricula

In the late 1960s, I became a moderator for examinations in Chemistry at the level of the then Certificate in Secondary Education (CSE). I learned about Bloom's (1956) *Taxonomy of Educational Objectives* and enthusiastically applied its six levels to the CSE examinations. My analyses showed a considerable bias towards 'knowledge' and 'comprehension' in the questions. There was a little 'application' and virtually nothing in the categories of 'analysis', 'synthesis' and 'evaluation'.

Shortly afterwards, I enrolled on an advanced diploma course in education, and for one of my assignments I undertook similar analyses of examinations in Chemistry at the progressively higher levels of General Certificate of Education (GCE) O-level, GCE A-level and first-year university. I naively expected to find a steady movement towards the higher levels of the Bloom Taxonomy, but instead the bias towards 'knowledge' and 'comprehension' remained much the same.

While I continued to have reservations about the relative failure of the assessments to incorporate much at the higher end of the Bloom Taxonomy, the attempt to apply the Bloom categories showed that, although the observed proportions of the lower categories were much the same across all the examinations, the compass of 'knowledge' and 'comprehension' was progressively extended. Students' progression was not simply linear, from 'knowledge' to 'evaluation', but spiral in form, revisiting the Bloom categories in progressively widening curricula.

I should have read Bruner's (1960) *The Process of Education* beforehand.

the students' normal level of performance. We discuss curriculum issues in more detail in Chapter 5.

Curriculum models and spirality

The division of an undergraduate programme into discrete levels that progressively and linearly develop academic knowledge, skills and competences through the three years of study represents an oversimplification of the learning and curriculum design process. In Bloom's *Taxonomy*, learning is structured into categories that represent degrees of difficulty. The assumption is sometimes made that a student progresses through these levels throughout a course of study. However, the highest level outcomes can be and are often achieved in the first year of an undergraduate curriculum. This is because most learning in higher education is developed through a curriculum model that approximates to a spiral (Bruner, 1960). With each re-acquaintance, the complexity of the engagement with the material increases and new material is related to previous learning. In a modular system, the application of the spirality may be dependent on specific module choices.

As curricula often contain several academic topics, there are potentially multiple spirals in operation at the same time. Curricular cohesion requires that, apart from optional modules chosen as 'widening' studies, there is bridging between spiral strands. In terms of spirality, two descriptions apply. There is spiralling 'out' to encompass more and more subject material, but also a spiralling 'in' as the detailed understanding of the material is refined. In setting out the framework of *The Psychology of Personal Constructs* George Kelly (1955) referred to both the extension and the definition of personal construct systems, which seems consistent with spiralling out and in.

What can quality assurance frameworks offer?

As we have seen, defining the second year in terms of the curriculum demands is complex. Repeated reappraisal of material and the development of multiple subject themes result in spiral, non-linear learning patterns of academic acquisition and application. So, if the academic identity of the second year cannot be inferred from learning models, what can quality assurance frameworks offer?

The UK may be regarded as one of the pioneers of quality frameworks; partial structures have been existent in the UK since the mid-1980s (Lester, 2011). In 1997, the UK National Committee of Inquiry into Higher Education Report (Dearing, 1997) recommended that the nature and level of academic standards be made more explicit. As a result, numerous quality documents were developed, including programme specifications, subject benchmark statements and a code of practice for the assurance of quality and standards. The purpose of these documents is to describe the characteristics of different academic levels and to provide a framework for measuring achievement using an outcomes-based approach where qualifications are awarded on the basis of the achievement of 'positively defined learning outcomes' (Quality Assurance Agency [QAA], 2013, p. 11). While this outcomes-based approach has been adopted across Europe, it is important to note that there have been criticisms of this method, particularly, in the context of its adaptability in supporting the demands of the European labour market (Mehaut and Winch, 2012). In this chapter, we ask whether is it possible to isolate the purpose and distinctiveness of the 'middle' educational years using these quality frameworks that aim to describe the relation between levels of learning in an educational system. Furthermore, we ask, can the academic identity of the second year of study be inferred through the language of the level descriptors?

The European Qualifications Framework (EQF): development of 'comprehensive' knowledge

The EQF is essentially a meta-framework designed to enable comparison of national qualifications systems in Europe and as such is a much-generalised communication tool. These qualifications descriptors make direct reference to knowledge, skills and competence. Level 5 in the EQF is equivalent to the second year of a three-year undergraduate programme. In this framework, the defining characteristic of Year 2 is 'comprehensive' with the final year as 'advanced'. Obviously, such generic definitions are limited in their application, but the terminology does provide an example of the challenge presented when attempting to define the second year. 'Comprehensive' suggests a broad acquisition of knowledge, skills and competences. A curriculum structure where the levels, or years, are defined with respect to the preceding or succeeding years is going to impact particularly on the characterisation of the middle years.

UK qualifications frameworks: development of 'criticality' in the second year

Two qualification frameworks exist in the UK, reflecting different undergraduate degree structures. In the England, Wales and Northern Ireland, higher education is structured according to the Framework for Higher Education Qualifications (FHEQ). This framework is developed and maintained by the QAA. In Scotland, the reference point is the Scottish Credit and Qualifications Framework (SCQF) which is managed by a partnership of national bodies including the QAA. In both frameworks, qualifications are referenced by qualification descriptors that describe levels of outcomes of learning. These outcomes are reviewed in the consideration of 'middle year' identity.

As with the EQF, the second year of an undergraduate degree programme is defined by the Level 5 descriptor in the FHEQ (QAA, 2013, A1, p. 10). The qualification descriptor identifies the nature and characteristics of this level of study. So how does the FHEQ define the second year? This period of study is seen to focus on critical engagement, effective communication and decision-making. We focus on 'criticality' and communication as examples of the challenges that the FHEQ (and, by extension, other frameworks) pose for curriculum designers. The FHEQ Level 5 descriptor makes two specific references to the development of a critical approach in terms of 'critical understanding' in the area of study and the capacity to 'evaluate critically' in approaches to problem-solving. The term 'critical' is not used in the Level 4 descriptor. Communication is a theme that runs through the FHEQ descriptors, but for Level 5, the emphasis is on effective communication to specialists and non-specialists rather than simply being able to communicate results. This suggests that a level of expertise differentiates Year 1 from Year 2 (or Level 4 from Level 5) students. Finally, decision-making is included in the qualities and transferrable skills expected of Level 5 students.

In a comparison of the FHEQ Level 5 descriptors with the Level 6, the critical evaluation and communication to non-specialists remain as key characteristics, but the context has been extended to place students at the forefront of their discipline, to appreciate uncertainty and ambiguity, and to apply decision-making skills to complex, unpredictable contexts. While the nature and challenge articulated in the FHEQ is clearly progressive, it could be argued that the transition from first to second year requires the development of significant study approaches and personal attributes for which the context is extended in the final year.

Therefore, while Level 5 can be differentiated from Level 6 using the FHEQ, it is actually quite difficult to separate Levels 5 and 6 (discussed in more detail in Chapter 5). This may account for the perceived stepping up required from the first year. However, it could be argued that critical engagement should be of Level 4 study. Should we not be demanding more of our students in their first year? If so, then we should see a more even intellectual progression through an undergraduate programme. It is also important to note that although these frameworks provide reference points for setting and assessing academic standards, they actually pay little attention to the processes of learning. This is because these structures specify outcomes and ends, while curriculum design focuses on process and means. These processes are discussed in detail in Chapters 3 and 4, where students' learning motivations through a programme of study are analysed and explained. This outcomes-based approach indicates how the curriculum should be constructed and implemented. However, focus groups' discussions with academic staff indicated that they felt that such frameworks were difficult to apply in the curriculum development process.

> And what does it mean to be second year standard? . . . I think we've conned ourselves a little bit with the descriptors.

> we are forced down the line of false descriptors which if you don't explain what level five means then that's going to lead to a dip. (Staff comments)

A comparative summary of requirements of learning across the three levels of undergraduate learning is shown in Table 2.1.

The SCQF

The SCQF is claimed to be one of the most successful and comprehensive frameworks in Europe (Raffe, 2011). In Scotland, students enter higher education a year earlier than they do in the rest of the UK. Consequently, a Scottish undergraduate degree programme is four years, with 'two middle years'. In the SCQF, the second and third years are referred to as Levels 8 and 9. In 2012 the framework was revised, and each level is described with reference to five categories: knowledge and understanding; practice; cognitive skills; communication, numeracy and information and communication technology (ICT); and autonomy, accountability and working with others. As with the FHEQ, a critical approach to study, as exemplified in statements around understanding, analysis and evaluation, is considered to be a crucial characteristic

Table 2.1 Comparison of the Framework for Higher Education Qualifications (FHEQ) across Levels 4–6

FHEQ Level 4	FHEQ Level 5	FHEQ Level 6
Knowledge of the area of study.	Knowledge and critical understanding of the area of study.	Systematic and coherent knowledge of the area of study.
Present, evaluate and interpret data.	Apply concepts. Demonstrate knowledge of main methods of enquiry. Understand limits of their knowledge and appreciate the impact of this on their findings.	Demonstrate a conceptual understanding based on current research.
Evaluate approaches to problem-solving.	Use range of techniques and undertake critical analysis and interpretation.	Engage in critical evaluation and determine a solution or range of solutions to a problem.
Communicate results accurately and reliably.	Communicate results to specialists and non-specialists.	Communicate results to specialists and non-specialists.
Develop new skills, particularly with respect to employment. Exercise personal responsibility.	Engage in skill development in order to assume significant responsibility. Exercise responsibility in decision-making skills.	Undertake professional training. Exercise initiative and personal responsibility. Demonstrate decision-making skills in complex and unpredictable contexts.

of these middle years ('critical' is used in descriptors for both Levels 8 and 9). Communication skills are focused on a range of audiences with presentation to more specialist audiences being a characteristic of Level 10, final-year students. In comparison with FHEQ, decision-making is not seen as a core characteristic of programmes. Autonomy and initiative are expressed explicitly in SCQF with Levels 8 and 9 being characterised by the ability to take a leadership role and deal with ethical and professional issues. As with FHEQ, the final year is defined by proficiency in the area of study and in handling aspects of unpredictability and more complex issues.

Within UK quality assurance frameworks, critical thinking is, therefore, a defining characteristic of the second or middle years of study. In focus groups with academic staff, the issue of criticality was never raised in discussions regarding the differences between the first and second years. There was no reference to the approaches students need to take. This could indicate an assumption that students, and perhaps also academic staff, see the curriculum more in terms of a holistic notion of 'progressive growth' rather than a linear progression through defined stages.

What can credit level descriptors offer?

In addition to the qualification frameworks in the UK, more detailed descriptions of the learning at each level exist in the form of credit level descriptors. These are generic statements used to determine the demand, complexity, depth and learner autonomy associated with a specific level of learning and achievement (QAA, 2008; European Qualification Framework Series note 4). They also link with academic, vocational or professional practice and detail the range and sophistication of the application of knowledge/skills into practice (Higher Education Credit Framework for England). The intention of these descriptors is to help write the learning outcomes and inform assessment criteria. Some credit level descriptors also make reference to the context of learning, the educational setting, as well as cognitive, practice and personal skills. They are therefore potentially useful in the determination of the diagnostic curriculum characteristics of the second year. However, a tension in these frameworks is between the requirements to provide statements of 'level' that are helpful in defining awards at different stage-points, for example, certificates, diplomas and degrees, and the desire to also reflect learning development through an academic programme of study. An example of a credit level descriptor is given in Box 2.2.

Quality frameworks and curriculum design

So what can quality frameworks offer in the design and delivery of the second-year curriculum? It is difficult to define this year without reference to the first and final year and even more difficult to differentiate the second from the final year in terms of the learning processes required in achieving the outcomes described

Box 2.2   England, Wales and Northern Ireland (EWNI) generic credit level descriptors

This framework supports the Framework for Higher Education Qualifications (FHEQ) (Higher Education Credit Framework for England: Guidance on Academic Credit Arrangements in Higher Education in England 2008) and describes the learning involved at a particular level of study.

At FHEQ Level 5 and Southern England Consortium for Credit Accumulation and Transfer (SEEC) Level 5, the learning associated with the descriptor reflects the ability to generate ideas, analyse information, exercise academic judgement and accept responsibility for determining individual or group outcomes. As with the qualification frameworks, these characteristics only really make sense when viewed in comparison with the Level 4 and Level 6 descriptions (see table below). From this table, it can be seen that, using these credit level descriptors, it is difficult to define the second year in terms of knowledge and skills and personal development. The development of an analytical approach differentiates Level 4 from Level 5, but as with the qualification frameworks, it is difficult to differentiate between Levels 5 and 6, reinforcing the step up to second year.

	Level 4	Level 5	Level 6
Knowledge and skills	Broad base of knowledge; employ skills	Command of specialised skills	Systematic and coherent body of knowledge; specialised skills
Evaluation, analysis and problem-solving	Evaluate information; determine solutions to unpredictable problems	Analyse and evaluate information; exercise significant judgement across broad range of functions	Critically evaluate evidence; exercise significant judgement in range of situations
Personal development	Take responsibility for nature and quality of outputs	Accept responsibility for determining and achieving personal and group outcomes	Accept accountability for achieving personal and group outcomes

in the frameworks. However, these frameworks do describe the step up in the second year in terms of developing more critical learning approaches. Criticality requires students to deconstruct concepts, actively interrogate data, and develop ideas and opinions. This increase in learning demands may have a significant impact on student behaviours. However, why criticality is characterised as a post–Level 4 approach is not clear. Criticality could be developed in the first year, and the academic complexities within which this learning behaviour is applied could increase within a programme of study, reflecting a spiral as opposed to linear curriculum. In Chapters 3 and 4, we see how students' learning motivations are affected by this increase in academic demand, and in Chapter 5, we discuss how to design the curriculum to militate against the decrease in student engagement sometimes seen in the middle years. From all quality frameworks, there appears to be an expectation for students to become critical learners in the second year of study, and this needs to be acknowledged and managed through an undergraduate degree programme.

Key issues

1   Defining the second year is difficult without reference to the first and final years. Both these years have well-understood academic characteristics, and the second year can be seen as a transitional or bridging year.
2   The experience of second-year students is strongly influenced by their first-year experience which may be determined by their entry qualifications. Students who have studied their undergraduate discipline at an advanced level at school may find themselves challenged academically for the first time in their second year.
3   Most curricula are not structured into discrete levels of learning, but are developed through a model that approximates to a spiral. In most undergraduate degrees, subjects are repeatedly revisited through the programme each time with increasing complexity.
4   Quality assurance frameworks offer an outcomes-based structure for differentiating between levels of study. Level descriptors identify the 'step up' to the second year through the development of critical approaches.

Notes

1 This may in part account for the weaker performances in higher education by students from fee-paying school backgrounds than by those from state schools where coaching for examination success is probably less prominent (see Higher Education Funding Council for England [HEFCE], 2003; 2005; 2014).
2 A useful summary is given by Krathwohl (2002).

Chapter 3

Shifting perspectives

*Elena Zaitseva, Clare Milsom and
Martyn Stewart*

'There is a shift in the way they act . . . '

> Last year I just kind of went with the flow and did the work, did the
> reading . . . I thought I was fine. There wasn't much pressure on you . . . But
> this year doing the same amount of reading, doing the work, marks are
> coming back lower. I was really upset . . . I went to one of the lecturers and
> said I don't know what I am doing wrong because I have done everything
> the same as I did last year and I have never got a mark as bad as this . . .
>
> (Extract from an interview with a second-year student)

Feeling lost, not understanding what is required in a particular assignment,
disappointed with performance, being confused and often frustrated: many
students who were interviewed as part of the project described the second year as
an 'emotional rollercoaster'. It was true of both groups – those who passed easily
through the first year, capitalising on their entry qualifications, and those who
found the first year a challenging experience.

Academic and support staff expressed similar views on the second-year
students' behaviour as a cohort. When asked about their experience of teaching
and supporting second years, staff frequently compared second-year students
with 'typical teenagers'. Many believed that problems and issues that second years
experience and their reaction to these problems are specific for the level of study.
As one member of staff observed,

> There is a shift in the way they act . . . The way in which that manifests itself
> is around a heightened sense of anxiety. It's a bit like in the first year they
> are sort of novice and they are young, and they are excited and then, in
> the second year . . . it's like the light in the tunnel is sufficiently far away to
> make that not an exciting goal, but the newness is not there. So I think they
> struggle a little more.

Academics characterised the second-year cohort in a variety of complex ways:
on the one hand, as being strategic, but very anxious; as better equipped to

undertake their studies, but frequently playing the system; as more confident in their ability to cope, but often complaining. It was suggested that the pressure of enhanced workload and 'marks being counted' (discussed in more detail in Chapter 5) often lead to certain patterns of behaviour, such as 'playing the game' or fault-finding:

> You will get the students who will swing the lead a bit, who will play the system, who will put in the personal mitigating circumstances because they know that opportunity is there . . . That's where you see that sort of behaviour established . . . Usually you very rarely see it . . . in year three.
>
> The second years . . . are known . . . amongst staff, as complainers. They are quite quick to complain about marks, about tutors, about feedback not being quick enough. They do start to be a bit more assertive, but also a bit more focussed [on their goals], I think.

Although these behaviour patterns were frequently observed by teaching staff, many academics were unclear about when and how the change in student behaviour occurred. They questioned conditions that led to a change in confidence and increased anxiety and the extent to which second-year students feel different from first-year students.

In Chapter 2, we saw how the middle years of the undergraduate degree lacked a positive definition. Here, we explore the first and second years as experienced and articulated by students, with a particular emphasis on perceptions of students in the middle phase of their studies. This chapter aims to identify any broad changes in attitude or focus and to characterise key shifts in behaviour (see Zaitseva *et al.*, 2013, for an extended version of this research).

'Visualising' collective voice of first- and second-year cohorts: using text analytics software to explore student priorities and attitudes

In order to find out what is important for first- and second-year students (as cohorts) and what elements of their experience they prioritise and find important, we decided to draw on a vast and readily available data source – free text comments from the institutional 'mirror' of the National Student Survey (NSS) for first- and second-year students. Although the Liverpool John Moores University (LJMU) 'mirror' survey response rates fluctuate around 28 per cent to 33 per cent, as more than half of those who respond leave comments, it represents the most comprehensive 'collective voice' of both cohorts gathered at a particular time point – the beginning of the second semester. The NSS asks students about their agreement with various statements related to different aspects of their course experience as well as inviting them to leave free text comments. As does the

NSS, the 'mirror' survey encourages students to comment on positive or negative aspects of the programme they would like to highlight, generating a considerable number of comments at an institutional level for analysis.

Given the large amount of textual data generated by the surveys, a text analytics software Leximancer (http://www.leximancer.com) was utilised for the analysis. The software automatically identifies concepts, themes (groups of concepts) and connections between them by data mining the text, and visually represents findings as a concept map (Smith and Humphreys, 2006). Based on an assumption that a concept, or word, is characterised by words that tend to appear in conjunction with it, the software measures how well a word is connected to other words, for example, how frequently they occur and/or appear together in the text. It then generates an interactive concept map that allows the researcher to visualise relationships between the words (concepts) and also see larger themes (strongly connected concept clusters).

In order to interpret the map and understand the meaning behind concepts and their connections, the concepts need to be manually examined in detail. By clicking on a concept, a researcher gets access to all instances (direct quotes) that contributed to its creation. Numerical parameters, such as relevancy weight ranking or level of connectivity, are also available to aid the interpretation of the concept map generated.

One of the advantages of this form of analysis is that it is highly inclusive and objective, with every sentence contributing to overall understanding. The concept map that emerges from this analysis captures 'the wisdom of crowds' and is in essence a text-driven, not researcher-driven, representation (Dodgson et al., 2008).

Leximancer is also able to identify sentiments associated with a concept. The sentiments are identified automatically by linking sentiment orientation, if available (e.g. certain adjectives, nouns or verbs indicative of positive or negative attitude), to the concept in the process of analysis, and calculating the statistical probability of the concept being mentioned in a favourable or unfavourable context. As students often leave positive as well as negative comments related to the same topic in surveys, gaining a sense of their attitude as a cohort to a particular element of their experience becomes problematic. The 'sentiment lens' helps with sentiment detection, identifying concepts as 'likely favourable' or 'likely unfavourable'.

Previous studies have demonstrated that the software can help mitigate researcher bias and increase objectivity when analysing large complex textual data sets, thereby increasing reliability and facilitating reproducibility of the findings (e.g. Penn-Edwards, 2010).

Comments left by two cohorts were analysed with the following aims in mind:

- To identify similarities and differences in the conceptual structure of comments provided by each level of study (e.g. the most important concepts, themes and their topology for each cohort).

- To examine the key concepts for each level and to surface level-specific connotations, including sentiments.
- To open up the discussion about the practical implications of the findings.

In addition to summarising key messages left by students in the surveys to illustrate the findings, where possible, we used quotes from various project interviews and focus groups undertaken during the lifetime of the project – to strengthen an argument or to present an alternative perspective.

The computer-aided analysis enabled us to undertake research in a much shorter, time-efficient way, with the possibility of reproducing the methodology for any other similar data sets. The output of the analysis also corresponded well with our research questions, as the software was able to graphically represent text as a concept map, showing the most important or 'relevant' concepts for the text creators.

In the following sections, concepts are shown in bold font (to distinguish them from regular words). Concept maps represented in the text were re-drawn from original maps generated by the software, with some peripheral concepts removed to improve clarity of the map.

First year: 'Feeling accepted and supported'

When free text comments left by first-year students were analysed by the software, the most relevant and most favourable concept, as indicated by concept map and numerical outputs, was **course** (Figure 3.1). In their comments, students often mentioned course in conjunction with **experience**, **work** and **feel**. **Course** was also situated in a close proximity to **interesting** and **teaching**. Exploration of the concept map showed that the majority of concepts surrounding course are experiential, often indicating emotion or attitude associated with a concept, all rated favourably. It suggests that course experience of students approaching mid-second semester of their first year of study is largely positive, with the affective domain playing an important role in student satisfaction.

Examination of the actual comments and student interviews supported this hypothesis: first-year students are likely to mention their course in a favourable context when they feel accepted and integrated into the learning community, supported by staff and peers, and engaged. One of the first-year students commented in an interview,

> I feel the tutors are very passionate about the course and always ensure that students feel secure but still manage to encourage us to push our boundaries.

Course experience was often mentioned in a positive, but generic (non-specific) way in both survey comments and in first years' interviews and focus groups:

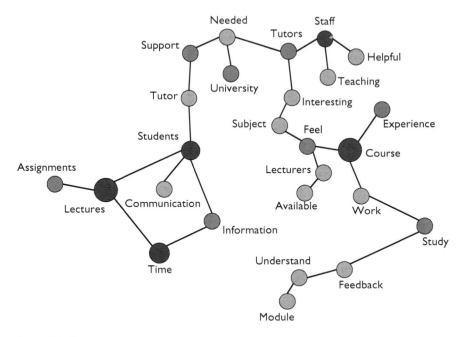

Figure 3.1 First-year concept map

So far I have had an extremely positive course experience.
It . . . has been a great experience so far and I look forward to what the future holds.

When asked to expand on specific elements of the course experience that were particularly good, students would give examples of activities and experiences that helped them in developing confidence, interest, social bonding or sense of belonging. Field trips and group work were mentioned most frequently, as in the following quotation:

There have been a lot of opportunities to work with different people on my course meaning that I now feel as though I know a lot of people and could easily find people to work with . . .

Students in the first-year focus groups often mentioned making friends, exploring a new environment and learning new life skills. All these activities were closely associated with a growth in confidence and positive perception of the course, supporting previous findings of Thomas (2012), Wilcox *et al.* (2005) and Yorke and Longden (2004).

The concept map also indicated that **teaching** (favourable concept) is closely positioned to the **course** and **experience** and connected to **interesting** and **subject** through **staff** and **tutors**. First-year students commented extensively on *passionate, engaging, inspiring, genuinely enthused lecturers and seminar leaders* who make their time at the university very enjoyable, often expressing their emotional disposition when leaving a comment.

University is also a favourably rated concept for this cohort, directly linked to **support** provided (specifically **tutor** support) and having **interesting** and **subject** in a close proximity:

> The staff have been both helpful and friendly in helping me settle at university . . . I feel that I have made the right choice to come to the university . . .

Feedback (favourable concept) is positioned between **study** and **understand**, suggesting the important role of the feedback in the student learning process. Survey comments and focus group discussions revealed that first-year students value feedback that is timely, helpful, and easy to understand and that boosts confidence:

> The feedback I received has given me the ability to understand what I am doing wrong and correct it.
>
> When looking back on the experience, I found that when I had done something well I got great feedback and this in turn boosted my confidence.

Concepts that were likely to be perceived negatively by the first-year students were associated with **lectures**, **module**, **assignments** and **time**. These and other elements of learning experience that involved uncertainty, lack of confidence or confusion were concentrated in the 'unfavourable corner' of the map (Figure 3.1, left-hand lower section).

The survey comments as well as interview responses suggested that experience of a 'traditional' academic lecture often alienates students, and in their second semester, many were still concerned about lack of interaction in large lecture rooms and a passive listening mode. This might be for a variety of reasons, including pace not being suitable for a particular student, the content being too overwhelming or the opposite, 'we are learning basics' and a perceived lack of challenge:

> The lecture theatre is huge . . . with many students . . . it's sometimes difficult to interact and become involved.
>
> Lectures . . . move at a pace which suits the lecturer and higher achievers . . .

Interview responses of some first-year students showed they were struggling with the pace of lectures but lacked the confidence to voice this:

They [lecturers] say things like do you want me to go slower? Well, no one is going to put their hand up and go 'yeah, actually please go slower', because half the people that are in there will be out in ten minutes texting away . . .

Interestingly, when lectures are interactive, first-year students – especially less confident ones – are not able to engage fully, being too anxious of giving a wrong answer:

I like the tutors asking questions and all that . . . [But] I just always feel like I am going to say the wrong thing and I'm shy and people are going to laugh at me . . . Everyone freezes, you have the answer on the tip of your tongue but you just don't want to put your hand up and say it because everyone just looks at you. Someone will say what you are thinking and I'll wish that I had said that now because it's right . . . It's so tense you are waiting for something to happen and then eventually the tutor goes ok then this is the answer, did you know that? And everyone sort of nods and mumbles . . .

First years' negative comments related to **assignments** were mainly concerned with lack of clarity or uncertainty about assignment requirements. Some students were critical about the **timetable**, clashing deadlines for coursework and also inconsistencies in teaching and assessment between different **modules**.

Thematic analysis demonstrated that **course** (favourable cluster of concepts) and **lectures** (unfavourable cluster) were the most semantically important themes in the Year 1 student comments.

Our findings supported arguments of Moore (1995), Parmar (2004) and Tinto (1994) showing that in their first year, students 'experience a real emotional journey' (Beard et al., 2007: 248), and their success is heavily dependent on aspects of social integration, which involve the affective dimensions of their engagement with higher education (Christie et al., 2005; Thomas, 2012).

When commenting on their educational experience in the mirror survey, first-year students were more likely to use language that involves expression of emotions, feelings or attitudes. Sentiment analysis also demonstrated that the majority of students (at least those who completed the survey or gave feedback on their course experience by other means) felt integrated and accepted by mid-second semester, which was reflected in the majority of the concepts being rated favourably.

Richardson (2003), who investigated the issues that UK students faced in their transition to university and the obstacles they encountered as they progress to Year 2 of their course, found that students may come to university with very fixed ideas about what to expect – this is related to how they would be taught, the anticipated workload and required academic skills, including completing assignments. Many replicate methods they had been taught at A level (Richardson,

2003) and, as we found in our case, some still find it difficult or are unable to overcome the psychological barrier of expressing their own opinion/answering questions when surrounded by dozens or even hundreds of other students on the course.

Second year: 'Enabling growth'

Analysis of the second years' comments demonstrated that **course** remains the most relevant and favourable concept for the Year 2 students (Figure 3.2). But, judged by its location on the concept map, **course** has different associations for the second years. **Learning**, a new favourable concept which is not present in Year 1 responses, is now directly linked to the **course** via **teaching** and **lecturers.**

Manual exploration of **learning**-related comments revealed a complex picture and various connotations of the concept. Second-year students were very appreciative of everything that enabled them to enhance learning opportunities. Phrases such as 'it has a positive effect on my learning', 'feel more confident in my learning', ' . . . were beneficial to my learning' are typical of many second years' comments, demonstrating students' attention to effectiveness of their learning and skills development. Second years also appreciate teaching and learning techniques that help them to achieve this. 'Great way of learning . . . ', 'simple yet effective way of learning', '[I liked this] . . . very interactive approach

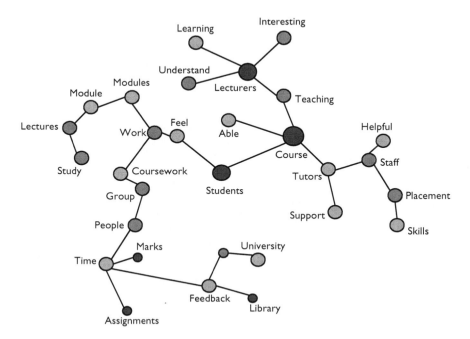

Figure 3.2 Second-year concept map

to learning . . . ' – these were frequently acknowledged by second years in their survey comments.

Practical learning and **placement**- (new concept linked to **skills**) based learning in particular were mentioned in a positive context: 'Placements are varied and encourage learning; practical trips helped to enhance our learning'.

At the same time, the peevish/demanding nature and strategic approach exhibited by the cohort – something that was noticed by academic and support staff – are also clearly seen in many learning-related comments:

> Learning absolutely nothing; this [student behaviour] is obstructive to my attention; [I wish] learning became easier and more useful; [These] factors were inhibiting or compromising our learning.

Learning as a concept lies within a close proximity to **understand** and **interesting**. Comparative analysis of the first and second years' comments demonstrated that student attention shifted from appreciation of excellent teaching in the first year to a recognition of how effectively the course was able to facilitate their understanding and learning – both in terms of their knowledge growth and know-how in optimising study approach:

> To enable growth and learning, feedback should be timely.
>
> Lots of little things [happened in second year] . . . Like we . . . realised how to do each report that you can get a really high course mark in and also little things . . . when you start to understand.

The word **able** (also a new concept), widely used in Year 2 positive comments, relates to the course and its ability to give students time, space and knowledge to understand, produce high-quality work, ask for help or to acquire professional skills:

> The practical side of my course has been of immeasurable value, as I have been able to gain a better understanding of something that I may not have understood simply by sitting in a lecture theatre . . .

Interestingly, while under increased pressure from a more challenging curriculum and assessment, some students attempt to adopt a more deep and structured approach, others seem to be becoming more strategic and are demonstrating a reactive behaviour. Focus on better performance is certainly seen to be more prominent, as the following interview quote illustrates:

> Last year I crammed all my note writing on the computer into about a month before the exams . . . Whereas this year I looked at my module that I have exams in and every time I go home after that lecture I'm typing it up in bullet form, so that when it comes to the exam I'm just printing it out and reading it. I haven't got to worry about typing anything up.

Importance of encoding in aiding student learning was explored by Howe (1974). Taking notes in class, as shown by the research, is an indicator that learners are alert to the content and able to extract information that is useful to them (ibid.). Structured and conscientious learning becomes more prominent in the second year, and 'external' pressures may be contributing, in part, to the changing learning strategy, as indicated below:

> In the first year . . . a lot of people mentioned, oh these aren't going towards your final degree mark. So you weren't sort of that worried if you got a low mark whereas in the second year – oh crap, this is going towards your final mark – which made you panic a little bit and put some effort as well.

Growth in personal confidence and better engagement with their learning in the second year was frequently mentioned in student interviews. Students commented on 'getting more comfortable asserting yourself', 'getting your voice out there' and 'feeling a lot more relaxed around staff'.

The second year was also associated with more independent and self-directed learning. Undertaking optional modules, especially when carefully selected, was seen as an opportunity to better engage with a particular area, talk to tutors and generally be more proactive in studying the subject of their choice. Together with gaining more confidence, second-year students start suggesting how their learning could be enhanced even more:

> It would be helpful to set aside a short amount of time at the end of the lecture to sum up the session's key themes . . . Having a structure and reflecting on the learning that has taken place would be a great way for students to then plan their own study time.
>
> The trips away should be made longer, a week, instead of three days. This way we will be able to learn even more and improve on previous skills that we already have.

While the second-year experience for many students coincided with a re-affirmation of purpose and goals and triggered reflection on their progress, for some the process of realisation and understanding of requirements and time and effort needed to perform well took longer, with a steep learning curve often happening in second semester:

> I don't think we were prepared enough for the second year because there is a lot more expected of you and you don't realise. Your first couple of assignments you get marked on them but you are not [ready yet], you are still learning how to do various things . . .
>
> I attended all the lectures in the first year, I attended all the lectures in the second year but in the first year I just did what I had to do, I didn't necessarily read that many things, the journals and stuff . . . I did exactly

the same in the second year but I found that harder and had to change [my approach] eventually.

Mature students in particular were very vocal about the immaturity of some younger peers:

> First year it was like find your footing . . . Then second year was like . . . right we expect you to do it now, so get on and do it. And then . . . you saw some students just taking the initiative and doing it, and then some students acting like first year was extended. You can't just stay in the realm of 'it doesn't matter', you have to move on, take initiative and work it out yourself . . .

Lectures and **time** remain unfavourable concepts, but both acquired a different connotation. Lack or diminished opportunity for learning as a result of ineffective delivery becomes a prominent reason for dissatisfaction. Also distinctive to the second-year comments were expressed concerns when timetabling did not maximise their ability to balance their studies, part-time work and social life:

> Students want to study, but when you have a three-hour gap between lectures how long can you wait around?
> The timetable was awkward for a commuting student like myself to get to and from the lectures as they were very sporadically set out.

When relevance weight (frequency of appearing in the text and connectivity with other words) of the first- and second-year concepts are compared, it could be seen that the relevance of **feel** and **tutors** become lower in the second years, while **course**, **teaching**, **work**, **feedback**, **staff**, **time**, **lecturers**, **modules**, **university**, **assignments**, **study** and **library** become more relevant (Table 3.1).

One of the students commented about the library:

> Last year I could have got an essay done just sitting at my laptop, I didn't even go to the library last year, and this year I go once a week.

Experience, **information** and **communication** completely disappeared from the Year 2 concept map, while new concepts, not present in Year 1 responses, come into sight – for example, **placement** and **skills**. This could be a reflection of the curricular changes (e.g. introduction of placements in the second year or group work) but also suggests that second-year students are becoming more concerned with the applied side of their experience and development of practical skills, as indicated earlier.

Sentiment analysis suggests that in Year 2, the attitude to the key concepts such as **university**, **feedback**, **coursework** and **year** changes from favourable to unfavourable, and the likelihood of the concepts such as **module** and **timetable** being mentioned in a negative context becomes much higher (Table 3.2).

Table 3.1 Comparison of the main concepts and their relevance weight by year

Concept	Year 1 Concept relevance (%)	Year 2 Concept relevance (%)
Course	80	100
Lectures	66	56
Students	56	70
Staff	55	60
Tutors	54	40
Feel	52	41
Time	51	56
Lecturers	43	53
Helpful	40	33
Feedback	30	38
Teaching	24	30
University	16	22
Library	14	17
Group	n/a	16

University visibly changes its location on the concept map in Year 2, moving away from **support** and becoming more closely positioned to **time** and **feedback**-related concepts. Analysis of the **university**-related comments also revealed that for second-year students, **university** has a stronger association with the distribution of resources, such as information and communications technology (ICT) facilities and financial support (emergency and in the form of scholarships), and was often mentioned in relation to various policies and regulations:

> The university needs to consider its mature students more.
> I feel some of the changes . . . are not told to us students by the university, such as information about bursaries . . .

Feedback becomes a more prominent and relevant concept, but is often mentioned in the context of delays or a failure to guide further learning. It appears from the comments that second-year students are more concerned with feedback as a means for improvement and progression, rather than encouragement and affirmations, as first-year students:

> To enable growth and learning feedback should be timely . . .

Some interviewees gave examples of a strategic attitude to seeking feedback from staff:

> But [by your second year] you know which tutors you can get hold of by email if you need them there and then . . . But some of them aren't very

Table 3.2 Comparative table of sentiments associated with the key concepts in Years 1 and 2

Concept	Year 1 Sentiment	Year 2 Sentiment
1 Course	Favour	Favour
2 Experience	Favour	n/a
3 University	Favour	Unfavour
4 Feedback	Favour	Unfavour
5 Coursework	Favour	Unfavour
6 Teaching	Favour	Favour
7 Staff	Favour	Favour
8 Tutors	Favour	Favour
9 Library	Favour	Favour
10 Support	Favour	Favour
13 Subject	Favour	n/a
15 Communication	Unfavour	n/a
16 Information	Unfavour	n/a
17 Assignments	Unfavour	Unfavour
18 Tutor	Unfavour	Favour
19 Lecturer	Unfavour	n/a
20 Lectures	Unfavour	Unfavour
22 Time(s)	Unfavour	Unfavour
23 Module	Unfavour	Unfavour
24 Timetable	Unfavour	Unfavour
26 Skills	n/a	Favour
27 Lecturers	Favour	Favour
28 Feel	Favour	Unfavour
32 Students	Unfavour	Unfavour
36 Group	n/a	Favour
38 Placement	n/a	Favour
39 Learning	n/a	Favour

good at emailing back, so you know you are better off just going to see them because they are better at giving you feedback that way . . .

Comments related to **module** indicate that badly organised modules and modules not contributing to learning and progression attract most negative entries:

In one particular module, coursework feedback was delayed, meaning that feedback could not be used by students to help with future assignments . . .

When thematic composition was explored, **course** (favourable) and **time** (unfavourable) were the most semantically important themes for the second-year students.

Establishing identity, purpose and developing autonomy: concluding remarks

Insights into student experiences, expectations and outcomes on each stage of their learning journey and understanding what enables successful transition from first to second year and beyond were the second-year experience project's key research aims. An undergraduate degree is a long journey for students with all sorts of implications 'if relationships with the university or with "inner self" break along the way' (Morgan and Brown, 2010: 50). Being aware of what is important for both cohorts, what their attitudes are to various aspects of their experience and what factors are driving second years' contradictory behaviour is imperative in order to better manage student expectations, provide additional guidance or support and ensure their success.

Comparative analysis of Years 1 and 2 concept maps generated by the software revealed that although there were some similarities in the conceptual structure of comments provided by both cohorts, there were distinctive differences in relation to where the main concepts were located and how they were defined. The analysis also highlighted different associations with other concepts and concept clusters across the two cohorts. Our findings presented in this chapter are similar to those of Richardson (2003), who found that many students appeared to be surprised at the increase in workload in Year 2 and felt they were unprepared for the extra demands that were placed on them. Some were not altogether confident that they knew what was required of them in their second year. Interviews demonstrated that students prone to slump were most likely adopting 'surface' approaches, waiting till 'crisis struck' and showing a higher level of dissatisfaction with the key elements of their learning experience.

Concept maps illuminated aspects of the learning experience that are important to students at different stages of their learning journey. The changes in student development, goal orientation and satisfaction by year were identified through differences in the language used and, subsequently, in the conceptual picture of their university experience.

Our findings revealed that students move from affectively oriented goals in the first year to a second year's cognitive and strategic stage which is driven by performance. This is generally supported by student development theory (Baxter Magolda, 1992; Rainey and Kolb, 1995). Chickering and Reisser (1993) also suggested that establishing identity, purpose, developing competence and autonomy were the most important areas of development for second-year students, while Lieberman and Remedios (2007) showed a shift in goal orientation from mastery to performance in the second year.

Change in student attitudes and priorities reflected in the emergence and strengthening from Year 2 of concepts associated with assessment such as marks, assignments, feedback, coursework and time, was accompanied by a shift in sentiment (they all become unfavourable concepts). Skills and practical, experiential learning start to gain more recognition in the second year and continue to be associated with a high course satisfaction in the final year (Zaitseva *et al.*, 2013).

In their literature review on first-year experience (predominantly an Australian context), Bowles *et al.* (2011: 64) state that 'for a significant number of students the first-year university experience is neither satisfying (in terms of personal fulfilment) nor successful (if academic achievement is the measure'. Based on our findings, we would argue that second year not only serves a 'true' identifier/ indicator of the first-year experience but also generates a new level of challenges that need to be addressed to ensure student success at each level of study. These challenges as well as their implications for curriculum design and student support will be explored in Chapters 5 and 6.

Chapter 4

Psychological orientations to learning in the second year

Martyn Stewart and Sue Darwent

Changing minds

The three or four years of an undergraduate degree can be an important period of self-discovery and growth for many students: living away from home for the first time, building new friendships, committing to their chosen subject, learning how to self-manage time and workload, discovering new interests and managing financial pressures. Student life presents a rich tapestry of experiences, opportunities and challenges, and it should be no surprise that motivation, confidence, emotion, anxieties and other dynamic facets of the individuals' make-up go through constant flux over the period of their course.

There is a surprising lack of research into how such factors vary across the different stages of the degree. Many educational studies of individual variation measure approaches to studying. Typically, they assume a degree of stability and type behaviours are characterised. For example, students are often identified as adopting a tendency towards 'deep' or 'surface' study approaches, having low or high self-efficacy, or motivated intrinsically for self-understanding or extrinsically for some related purpose.

The previous chapter signalled some of the shifts in focus that occur for students as they progress through their time at university. This chapter narrows this focus to students' psychological dispositions and considers measures of their variation at different stages of their degree. Findings generated from the *Second Year Experience* project are related to international research to identify characteristics and themes of general relevance. From these results, we shall discover how the second year appears pivotal in influencing students' motives for studying and their psychological orientation. Deeper questions are raised about the goals and motives for taking up higher education and the extent to which behaviours are influenced by messages and cues from institutions.

From learning to performance

What drives a student's approach to studying over the duration of their degree? Understanding individuals' motives for studying is significant; research has long recognised the importance of motivation in influencing academic achievement and directing how learners approach their work.

Motives for studying vary among individuals. They seem also to change over time. Most students will probably enter university having given their choice of subject much thought. They may enter with an embryonic image of themselves as a future engineer. They may be following the family tradition of working in architecture. They may just want a qualification. When we market degree courses to prospective students, we focus on the discipline and emphasise the exciting opportunities that lie ahead were they to choose that subject. Evidence from research carried out as part of the *Second Year Experience* project confirms existing findings which show that study goals change at different stages of the degree. These changing motives can have a marked effect on attitudes towards study and consequently on the study strategies employed.

In order to investigate study motivation, a conceptual framework is needed. The main framework for conceptualising motivation in educational contexts today is called achievement goal theory. The theory can be traced back 50 years and has been investigated extensively in recent decades (Atkinson, 1964; Dweck and Elliott, 1983; Nicholls, 1984; Ames, 1992; Elliot and McGregor, 2001; Ciani *et al.*, 2011). Achievement goal theory recognises two fundamentally different motivations that appear to drive student behaviour, that provide a purpose for studying and that define measures of success. The first is a learning motivation: more technically described as a mastery goal orientation. The second is a performance goal motivation. Table 4.1 highlights the differences.

In straightforward terms, students motivated to achieve mastery in their subject are driven mostly by a desire to learn and overcome challenges. They are motivated to achieve competency and typically define their own standards, judging success against these. Usually intrinsically motivated, students often set out to prove something to themselves. In contrast, there is achievement as performance. A student driven by performance goals focuses on publically demonstrating their ability, with success evaluated through comparison with the achievements of others. The focus is less on learning for learning's sake, but more on achieving good grades. A fourfold organisational framework has been developed (Pintrich, 2000;

Table 4.1 Contrasting motives for studying according to achievement goal theory

Learning (mastery) goals	Performance goals
I'm here to learn – I want to master the subject	I'm here to do well – I want good marks
I love the challenge – I get a kick out of solving problems	I love being the best – I love being ranked first
I want to be good at it	I want to prove to others that I'm good at it
I'm working to my own targets	I judge success by comparing to others
I'm setting out to prove something to myself	I'm setting out to prove something to others

Elliot and McGregor, 2001) that not only differentiates between learning and performance motives but also recognises negative drives for each. Thus, mastery-avoidance occurs where the student is motivated out of concern for not understanding a concept or not achieving valued standards. In performance-avoidance, the motivation is to avoid appearing incompetent in front of others. Crucially, the two orientations are not mutually exclusive; students may adopt different motives simultaneously. So students may be motivated both by their intrinsic interest in mastering their subject and by being competitively driven to be top of their class.

So why draw this attention to motivational focus? Recent studies have identified strong associations between learning goals and other educational outcomes. For example, it has been shown that students motivated towards mastery and achieving understanding are found to adopt deeper approaches to studying (Pintrich, 1999; Zusho et al., 2003; Trigwell et al., 2013). They are likely to explore their subject more deeply out of choice and to go beyond narrow specifications set out by tutors. Strong learning or mastery motivation has been found to positively predict interest (Harackiewicz et al., 2002) and good grades (Simons et al., 2004; Smith et al., 2012). It has also been associated positively with conceptual change learning (Ranellucci et al., 2013), particularly important in higher education because students often enter their studies with outdated prior knowledge that requires deconstructing. Finally, Trigwell et al. (2013) demonstrated that students who conceived learning to be about developing understanding were more likely to perceive their workload as appropriate. This is significant, given that academic success is often linked to time-on-task (Chickering and Gamson, 1987).

Links between performance motives, study strategies and achievement are less clear; as the focus is on grades, students are more likely to adopt surface learning strategies such as memorisation and rehearsal. They are likely to narrow focus to those aspects of a course perceived as contributing to achieving good grades and to place lower value on that learning that does not 'count'. Performance goal motives have been found to negatively predict conceptual change (Ranellucci et al., 2013). Again, this may be significant at advanced levels of the degree where there is a focus on developing higher level outcomes such as criticality (see Chapter 2).

Few studies have examined changes in motivational orientations over time, particularly over the longer life cycle of an undergraduate degree course. Some studies report stability for individuals (Phan, 2009; De Clercq et al., 2013). Ciani et al. (2011) have recently demonstrated that achievement goals vary over the course of a semester and found both mastery- and performance approaches to decline. The fall in mastery-approach was greatest where students perceived the teacher as controlling.

Over the longer duration, Lieberman and Remedios (2007) studied undergraduate students at a UK university and found that a mastery-approach was stronger for students in their first year of study and lower for students at more advanced stages. Similarly, in Norway, Bråten and Olaussen (2005) reported a fall in mastery goals into the beginning of the second year. Comparable results were replicated with Russian students across four years of study (Remedios *et al.*, 2008), identifying a similar decline in motivation to master the subject with academic level. Significantly, these researchers found that interest and enjoyment dropped as the desire to master the subject fell.

Two studies were undertaken as part of the *Second Year Experience* project to investigate this phenomenon further. Using Elliot and McGregor's *2 × 2 Achievement Goal Framework* measure, Stewart *et al.* (in press) surveyed 200 students across two courses (Geography and Outdoor Education; Year 1, n = 65; Year 2, n = 68; Year 3, n = 67). Descriptive data revealed that, as with the earlier studies, mastery-approach declined after Year 1 (see Figure 4.1). In contrast, performance-approach goals increased, but by a smaller amount. More detailed statistical testing to determine the magnitude of these changing motives found the decline in mastery goals to be strongest, with the sharpest and statistically significant decline occurring between Years 1 and 2.

In a separate study, Darwent and Stewart (2014) assessed a fuller range of psychological variables across samples of Year 1 and Year 2 students on five courses (n = 521). A suite of psychometric instruments measured achievement goals, stress, academic self-efficacy, autonomous learning, metacognition and control-of-learning beliefs. Three of the sample courses were identified as 'slumping' courses because they showed a consistent performance dip in the middle year (characterised by average grade). Only mastery-approach was found to show a statistically significant difference by level, again declining from Year 1 to Year 2. In fact, of the ten psychological measures used in this study to characterise profiles between slumping and non-slumping courses, only the mastery-approach scale showed a statistically significant difference: students on the two 'non-slumping' courses reporting higher motives to master the subject in Year 2.

Collectively, these findings paint a significant and perhaps a somewhat pessimistic picture of a shift away from learning motives after the first year. This is less than half way through their course. This is significant because of the known associations with other positive outcomes such as interest and enjoyment, but also adoption of deeper study strategies and conceptual change learning. The latter is particularly relevant to the higher levels of an undergraduate degree. This shift is also recorded in some of the findings from the survey free-text comments examined as part of the project (see Chapter 3), with strong reference to course interest in the first year followed by emphasis on strategic learning and performance in the second year.

Lieberman and Remedios (2007) and Remedios *et al.* (2008) proposed that increasing pressure to do well at advancing stages of the course could be undermining students' interest in their studies. As students progressed, they needed to be more instrumental and pragmatic to focus on grades. This would certainly be supported by comments expressed through our focus group interviews, which reveal the tension between learning and performance reflected in the choices that second-year students face:

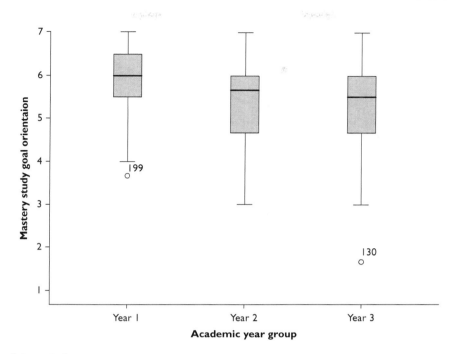

Interpretation

Mastery scores determined from a 7-point Likert scale assessing the extent to which participants agreed or disagreed with a statement measuring mastery goal orientation. High scores represent high learning goals.

The box-plots show the spread of data for each Year cohort divided into quartiles. Thus the lower line represents the spread of scores for the lowest scoring quarter of the sample, the lower and upper halves of the grey box representing the middle quartiles (25–50% and 50–75%) and the upper line representing the top scoring quarter.

Figure 4.1 Box plot showing mean scores for learning orientation across a sample of 200 geography and outdoor education students (Year 1, n = 65; Year 2, n = 68; Year 3, n = 67)

[in the second year there are] more module choices – you can pick something you are more interested in. But it's . . . what do you base your module choices on? Do you base it on something you want to learn? Something you are interested in? Or do you base it on something you think you will get a good mark in?

Mine was more leaning towards what I thought I could get a good mark in, so some of the stuff I didn't particularly like but I found easier.

However, it is also likely that the shift away from learning could be explained by students becoming more deeply engaged in the broader university experience, with competition on time increasing. As one student in the interviews noted, by the second year I'd only just sort of grasped it [understanding of university] and then just sort of decided to experience university life. And instead of the first year doing it, I did very much of it in the second year. And hence probably the less important academic stuff went out of the window a bit for me.

It is perhaps inevitable that students will want to maximise their success at university. What is concerning is that this significant deflection away from learning goals appears to occur so early.

Taking (and losing?) control

Students who are aware of, and can think about, their thinking are likely to be actively engaged in their learning, use more effective learning approaches and so attain greater success (Evans *et al.*, 2003; Vrugt and Oort, 2008). This ability, labelled metacognition, is, along with motivation, part of the comprehensive self-regulated learning framework developed by Pintrich (2004), which is 'crucial to student learning and academic performance', according to De Clercq *et al.* (2013). Metacognition is where the student is aware of their own thought processes and has the ability to self-observe and reflect, and then use these observations to guide practice and shape actions (Credé and Phillips, 2011). We have just considered study motivation; metacognition provides a bridge between motivational goal-setting and study behaviours. There is evidence from the study project that shifts in metacognition also occur from the first to the second year of study.

It is useful to think of self-regulation as comprising two dimensions: regulatory *processes* such as metacognition and self-efficacy, and self-regulatory *strategies*, for example, time management and effort regulation. As with learning goals, positive associations have been identified between students' self-regulation ability and deep learning approaches, including relating, contextualising and criticising, which aim at gaining comprehension (De Clercq *et al.*, 2013; Vermetten *et al.*, 2001). This appears particularly important in the second year because the quality frameworks focus on the development of criticality in defining the step up to this stage (see Chapter 2), when students are expected to use deeper learning processes in their reading and research.

On entry to university, there is evidence that students expect to work more independently (Childs and Spencer, 2002), but the shift toward personal responsibility is also anxiety-provoking. Learner autonomy includes dimensions such as motivation to learn, taking responsibility, gaining enjoyment from learning, managing time well and planning effectively, working alone, persevering in the face of difficulty and not overly procrastinating, according to Macaskill and Taylor (2010). Some students will experience difficulty in adapting to this, but, as recognised by interviews with staff and wider research, there is a general *expectation* that by Year 2, students will have successfully achieved the transition.

However, high levels of academic support provided in the first year to help ease the transition to university can leave students unprepared for the greater degree of self-regulation and independence expected in Year 2 (see Chapter 6). As one Year 2 student explained:

> Last year the tasks were set out more straightforward and they told you, basically, what to put in. Obviously you had to write it in your own way but this year it seems more independent. You have got to go away and decide what you want to put in.

A Year 3 student reflected back that excessive support in Year 1 had left students unprepared for the transition to Year 2:

> I think maybe the spoon feeding [in the first year] – that's not a cushion for someone to fall back on because you haven't put the work in.

Two of the scales used by Darwent and Stewart (2014) to investigate psychological profiles between 'slumping' and 'non-slumping' programmes as part of the *Second Year Experience* project measured aspects of self-regulation. These were Pintrich *et al.*'s (1993) *Metacognition* scale and the *Autonomous Learning* scale of Macaskill and Taylor (2010). Results revealed no differences between 'slumping' and 'non-slumping' courses for Year 1 students. However, both metacognition and autonomous learning beliefs were found to be higher among Year 2 students in the non-slumping courses, and conversely, to reduce somewhat from Year 1 to Year 2 for students on 'slumping' courses.

This is significant, thinking back to some of the quotes from students about their sense of preparedness. In courses where students reported higher scores in self-regulation in the second year, these coincide with improved mean performance. This could indicate that these courses were doing something positive by Year 2 that prepared these students to step up to the new demands at this level.

Further evidence for differences in self-regulatory behaviour was found in the study by Stewart *et al.* (in press). This looked at issues of self-regulation from a different perspective, the tendency towards procrastination, which is usually considered a form of self-regulatory failure (Wolters, 2003; Steel, 2007). Not all procrastination tendencies are negative, as many individuals purposefully delay tasks (Corkin *et al.*, 2011). However, it is more commonly 'maladaptive', where tasks are deferred, which reflects difficulties in self-managing time or study (Figure 4.2).

The study by Stewart *et al.* (in press) measured maladaptive procrastination tendency across the Geography and Outdoor Education courses (n = 200) using the *Tuckman Procrastination Scale* (Tuckman, 1991). Box plots (Figure 4.3) show the relative differences in procrastination tendency reported across the three levels. Year 1 students demonstrated a lower tendency towards procrastination, while scores for students in Years 2 and 3 were similar. Further testing confirmed that the jump from Year 1 to Year 2 was of statistical significance. Correlations with goal orientations

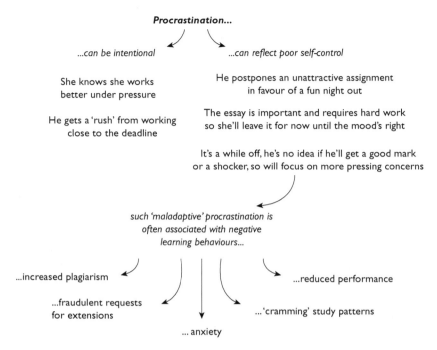

Figure 4.2 Overview of forms of procrastination as purposeful or a form of self-regulatory failure

Notes
For self-regulatory failure, negative study behaviours with known associations are shown.

measured in the same study identified a significant link with mastery goals: students with a stronger learning orientation being less likely to procrastinate, confirming links between motivation and self-regulation found in other studies (Lee, 2005; Haarala-Muholen *et al.*, 2011). Again, recognising the wider implications of this is significant, as Wäschle *et al.* (2014) explain how procrastination and low achievement goals can reciprocally amplify one another. Students can find themselves in a troubled cycle delaying work because of suppressed motivation.

Increased procrastination as students step into Year 2 may be a symptom of struggling to cope or self-regulate time or workload. Psychological research in the field of procrastination frequently relates the behaviour to the perceived importance of a task. Wolters (2003) found that procrastination tendency was greatest where tasks were perceived to be 'costly', requiring hard work. Steel (2007) describes the phenomenon of 'temporal discounting', where procrastination becomes more likely when the value of larger, more distant, rewards becomes subordinate to smaller, more immediately available rewards: 'The *potential* reward for doing that important piece of coursework (good grade)

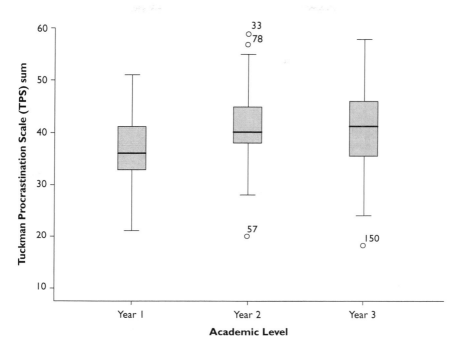

Interpretation

Procrastination scores determined from a 4-point Likert scale assessing the extent to which participants agreed or disagreed with a statement measuring maladaptive procrastination tendency. Higher
scores represent high tendency toward procrastination.

As with Figure 4.1, the box plots show the spread of data for each Year cohort divided into quartiles. Clearly there is a marked difference after Year 1 evident from this data.

Figure 4.3 Box plot showing mean scores for procrastination tendency across the
same sample of 200 geography and outdoor education students described in
Figure 4.1

is some way off, and all my friends are going out on the town tonight which will
almost guarantee a good time. No contest!' For those second-year students who
indicated that they became more deeply engaged in sport or social activities, or
simply partying more, this may be significant.

It may also be significant that assessment tasks at Year 2 have an elevated
importance, with grades now 'counting' towards the final award (Chapter 2).
The value of this work is now greater; the stakes are higher.

Anxiety and coping with stressors

We have already seen, both in the previous chapter and here, that students attach
greater significance to assessed work and appear to shift motivation more to
achieving good grades as they progress through their studies. Based on interviews

with Year 2 students, this performance focus appears to be accompanied by elevated anxiety and stress. This is significant as heightened academic stress has been found to be associated with lower course grades or failure to obtain a degree (Andrews and Wilding, 2004; Vaez and Laflamme, 2008). Often stress will be mediated by students' coping strategies (Struthers *et al.*, 2000), learned resourcefulness (Akgun and Ciarrochi, 2003) or personal appraisal of problem-solving ability (Baker, 2003).

Second-year students report stress not only associated with academic work, but also with personal relationships, living arrangements and balancing study and work responsibilities. In a study of undergraduate psychology students (n = 6,053), Smyth *et al.* (2008) found that over half reported experiencing at least one significant adverse life event, which could contribute to poorer academic performance. Andrews and Wilding (2004) showed that, among UK students who had previously shown no indicators of anxiety on enrolment, by the mid-point of the degree there was a 9 per cent increase in depression and a 20 per cent increase in anxiety at a level deemed clinically significant. These increases were attributed largely to financial and relationship pressures. Scott and Cashmore (2012) also found that such pressures were often encountered as students were coming to terms with living in rented accommodation for the first time in their second year. However, they also found living in rented accommodation could work to students' advantage and support studies; it was usually quieter than communal halls, and strong peer support could be provided from housemates.

One of the psychometric scales used by Darwent and Stewart (2014) as part of the *Second Year Experience* project measured stress across the five 'slumping' and 'non-slumping' courses (the ten-item *Perceived Stress Scale* of Cohen *et al.*, 1983). No *significant* differences in stress levels were found between Year 1 and Year 2 students, which appears contrary to findings from the interview studies; however, students on the 'slumping' courses did demonstrate higher stress scores, just not at a level of statistical significance. Second-year students with lower marks from the first year (40–49% and 50–59%) had noticeably higher perceived stress scores than students with the highest marks (70% or greater), again suggesting an association with performance. Further statistical examination of interactions found that low stress was associated with high self-efficacy: this was one of the strongest correlations in the study and again indicates the importance of developing students' confidence in their abilities. Students with higher stress scores also tended to be motivated by avoidance goals, driven by the 'fear' of not understanding the subject, concurring with findings of Elliot and McGregor (2001). All of this indicates that there exist important links between anxiety, students' sense of personal control, motivation and avoidance strategies.

So what are the sources of anxiety? Based on the interviews with Year 2 students, anxiety was frequently associated with workload and the knowledge that grades now 'counted' to the final degree award:

> In the first year there was the issue a lot of people mentioned, 'oh these aren't going towards your final degree mark', so you weren't sort of that

worried if you got a low mark, whereas in the second year ' . . . this is going towards your final mark' – which made you panic a little bit as well.

Same for me – more stress, stress and pressure on you, knowing that its 30%? It goes to your third year whereas first year was just . . .

However, it was clear that students had different coping strategies with some students motivated by pressure; as one Year 2 student commented:

I prefer to constantly be under stress and have stuff to do than be given a week off and risk not doing anything.

Another Year 2 student commented:

We've been told to start doing stuff for next year and we haven't even finished the second year yet. So obviously we are all . . . I wouldn't say we are stressed out in the room, but we have quite a lot of work on at the moment and we are getting told about stuff for next year as well. That's in the back of your mind so you are thinking we've got all this work in second year and we want to start doing some third year work now.

This suggests that, when making connections to future study, caution is needed not to present additional pressure as students are coping with existing work. This may also reflect perceptual differences where academics tend to think over the longer term unlike students who typically think within a more immediate time-frame (Price *et al.*, 2010).

As cited above, there are some indicators from the interviews that some anxieties may be generated by the messages that teachers or institutions are sending out about the importance of assessed work, and it is valuable to reflect on how easily teachers' behaviours can cause a shift in students' attitudes towards a task. Figure 4.4 provides a simple analogy in a different context to illustrate how relatively minor changes in teachers' behaviour and context can generate disproportionate anxiety among students.

It may be worthwhile to reflect whether, in relation to the second year, our own discourse changes and creates a similar effect to mobilise a shift towards performance goals. Chapter 5 will examine such issues in more detail to consider how our classroom environments may create goal structures that influence how students view their work.

Self-efficacy and confidence

So far, this chapter has considered motivational orientation, self-regulation and anxiety. Underlying these factors is the students' sense of self-efficacy. Students with greater belief in their abilities, and with greater confidence in themselves, are likely to initiate more things, apply additional effort and persevere in the face of

---

How to manufacture anxiety: an analogy

As part of an undergraduate geology course, two of the authors ran a week-long residential fieldtrip for first-year students to the Isle of Arran off the coast of Scotland. This course had run for many years. One day of the trip included a study of rock formations along the coast and involved a 3-mile coastal walk. At the end of the day, the field party would then face a return walk back to the accommodation that involved walking over a large hill. Students would set off on this walk on their own, at their own pace, with the tutors remaining at the rear in case students required any assistance. The uphill walk was not particularly strenuous, there was a clear wide path, the weather was often excellent and the views from the hill were breathtaking. For many students this walk was the highlight of the trip, a beautiful day out.

One year there were a few slight changes. The geology department's health and safety policy was more rigorous and greater emphasis was spent in the field on encouraging students to assess situations to identify safety risks. Students were also required to carry high visibility vests. The weather was drab on the day of the coast/hill walk: it became clear that the students would need to walk over the hill shrouded in mist. Throughout the morning we, as tutors, drew attention to the later hill walk and the mist, the potential hazards that students may face on their walk back, and to the importance of wearing their safety vests. Discussions about the hill walk continued throughout the morning and we reassured students they wouldn't get lost.

Our intentions had meant to mitigate any slight concerns students may have had, but tended to have the opposite effect. By drawing attention to 'the problem' and repeatedly reassuring mild apprehensions, we were actually beginning to manufacture students' anxieties. By the time students reached the foot of the hill to start the return journey, many were genuinely concerned about the 'dangerous walk' that lay ahead. We had inadvertently turned a pleasant walk into something to worry about.

Lessons for the 'sophomore slump'?

By drawing attention to the fact that the second year 'now counts', highlighting the importance of assessment tasks, of reading assessment criteria and attending classes to do well, as well as raising awareness of dangers of collusion and plagiarism, are we fuelling a focus on assessment and racking up the anxiety? Are we balancing this with the positive messages about learning?

Figure 4.4 Influencing students' anxiety through teacher behaviour

difficulty. Perceived self-efficacy has been shown to make a useful contribution to predicting academic achievement (e.g. Lane and Lane, 2001; Lane *et al.*, 2004). Significantly, it has been found that for students who withdraw from university in their second year, a strong internal focus has been identified, with individuals more likely to focus on their own perceived inadequacies (Willcoxson *et al.*, 2011). As these authors explain, this is quite different from reasons given for withdrawal in the first year, where external factors are more likely to be blamed.

Self-efficacy is fundamentally a belief that individuals hold about their capabilities in different areas. Such a belief can be changed. Confidence in academic ability is influenced by past performance, but a number of mediating processes have an impact, according to Chemers *et al.* (2001). These include metacognition, setting challenging goals, having effective coping strategies, optimism and positive expectations. These authors found that confident and optimistic students tended to see the university experience as a challenge rather than a threat, and consequently felt less anxious, setting themselves more demanding goals.

This leads us to ask, can learning environments be structured to help students develop their efficacy beliefs? Malau-Aduli *et al.* (2013) attempted to discover if a remediation course for underperforming Year 4 and Year 5 medical students based on self-efficacy and self-regulation would be effective. Students attended a ten-week intensive course focusing on presentation skills, videotaped mock interviews, practice with other students, small clinical tutorials and individual and group feedback. The small mixed-methods study indicated that the students made substantial improvements in their academic and clinical performance and that self-efficacy increased significantly. We shall return to this issue in Chapter 5.

However, simply setting challenges for students and assuming that this will improve their self-efficacy is not sufficient, as Brooman and Darwent (2013) discovered when developing a novel transition process for first-year students. New students worked together in small groups, with support from experienced second-year peers, to investigate and produce a poster about a particular law topic. Despite the opportunity to regulate their own learning experience, rise to a challenge in a structured and supported environment, learn from role models and settle into the course in a less stressful way, average self-efficacy scores did not increase over the month. On further investigation, it appeared that male students' efficacy beliefs tended to increase and female students' beliefs tended to decrease. It was an important learning point: don't assume your interventions are working – find out for sure!

Returning to the Darwent and Stewart (2014) study conducted for this project, self-efficacy was measured utilising the 15-item *Academic Self-efficacy* scale of McIlroy and Bunting (2002). Findings revealed that self-efficacy correlated strongly and positively with the self-regulation and autonomous learning scales, and negatively with mastery-avoidance. Comparing the 'slumping' courses with 'non-slumping' courses, similar self-efficacy levels were found at Year 1, but higher self-efficacy was reported for second-year students on non-slumping courses. Again, comparing with the results for the metacognition and autonomous learning beliefs described earlier, these results show that where the students appear 'better equipped' mentally in Year 2, this corresponds with an improved grade profile.

Summary

Drawing this work together, it is clear that student psychologies are complex and the variables examined are interconnected. Differences in motivation, anxiety, self-regulation and confidence in ability have been measured and found to differ between courses that perform well in the second year with those that do not. The findings from research conducted as part of the *Second Year Experience* project concurs with those in wider studies. These variables are central to understanding students' engagement with their studies; recognition of the changing dynamics is important as it points to where curricular interventions and support strategies are needed, discussed in Chapters 5 and 6.

Based on our quantitative analyses, it is clear that the transition from the first to the second year is where the magnitude of changes appears to be greatest. This may indicate that the second year acts as a period of adjustment where the students adapt and learn to cope – not always successfully – ahead of the final stages of their study. In this case-study institution, as in most English three-year degree programmes, grades achieved in the second year start to count towards the final award. Knowledge that the stakes are higher in Year 2 may be a significant factor in causing attitudinal and behavioural shifts, although certainly the situation is more complex than this.

Focusing purely on what could be measured, the stand-out finding from the project evidence is the marked decline in students' desire to master their subject that takes place in Year 2. This variable change has the greatest magnitude in both the psychological studies conducted as part of the *Second Year Experience* project (Darwent and Stewart, 2014; Stewart *et al.*, in press) and was the most significant change recorded in the 11 variables measured across the two studies. This finding also replicates results from comparable research (Bråten and Olaussen, 2005; Lieberman and Remedios, 2007; Remedios *et al.*, 2008). Qualitative findings report an increase in attention to grades and assignments, but in quantitative measures, it is the shift in motivation away from learning goals that is the more significant. Part of the issue will undoubtedly be pressures elsewhere, as time demands from employment or leisure compete for students' attention. But there is strong evidence from interview comments that learning becomes devalued as attention shifts towards gaining good grades:

> I found doing the essays and coursework to be a lot more important than going to lectures and learning.
> I would definitely lean towards what assessment I preferred rather than what the module topic was.

Lieberman and Remedios (2007) and Remedios *et al.* (2008) explain this shift as a response to the pressure to get good grades, and feedback from students at our university indicate that this shift is linked to the fact that assessment now 'counts' towards the final degree classification. In the project institution, the second-year 'counts' for only 25 per cent of the final degree, but is still sufficient to influence how some students select modules, steering away from choosing topics of interest to those course units with more attractive assessment tasks.

Does it matter that students become more narrowly focused towards performance goals? Does it matter that learning 'for learning's sake' takes a back seat? We would argue that it does matter for a number of reasons. First, learning goals are associated with other positive learning outcomes important at university level and especially the higher levels: deep approaches to study, conceptual change approaches and a more accepting view of higher workloads. Second, performance goals can narrow the focus too much to specific course elements, usually assignments and lectures linked to assessed work, and devalue other parts of the course. Some studies have found that in complex learning domains, a narrow strategic focus on achieving performance goals can interfere with the wider learning process, inhibiting learning by making it less likely the individual attempts alternative methods that could help perform the task (Locke and Latham, 2002). If we learn from wider studies of over-prescribed performance goal-setting, we learn of systematic harm that can arise, with increased likelihood of neglect of non-goal areas, reduced intrinsic motivation, corrosion of organisational culture and rise in unethical behaviour (Ordóñez et al., 2009).

Third, and perhaps most importantly, are we doing enough to inspire interest in the subject and value learning if students' interest in the subject apparently declines so soon? We are now deep in a performative culture across education and some of the problems may in part be rooted earlier. This is indicated by one student reflecting on testing at school:

> They make out your SATs[1] are going to be your absolute future and then your GCSEs[2] and then you're thinking, oh that's going to be my future, if I fail my GCSEs I've failed at life. And then you're in college and you think, oh I've got to pass this and then if I don't I failed that and then at university they are doing the exact same thing . . .

It need not take much of a cue to emit signals that can have a material and damaging impact on how students approach their work and place value on learning. We shall consider in Chapter 5 the influence that teachers and institutions play in shaping the learning environment and culture.

It is also clear that developing students' confidence in their abilities, especially to self-regulate, is of particular importance for entering the second year. This is to ensure students are armed with the tools to cope with the increased demands, workload and uncertainties encountered in the second year. For the next chapter, this will be a particular focus.

In conclusion, a complex range of issues and relationships are highlighted by these psychological studies. Every student is different. Each individual will have different motives. Some students will be better placed to manage their situation, be more resilient to pressure or adapt their approach to seize or navigate around obstacles. It does appear that the second year of the undergraduate degree is pivotal and where many changes – particularly associated with motivational focus, self-efficacy and self-regulation – are especially marked. The following chapters will consider how universities, academic departments and individual teachers can best guide students through this demanding stage of the degree.

Notes

1 SATs are Standard Assessment Tests in UK schools.
2 GCSEs are academic qualifications taken usually at the age of 16.

Chapter 5

Positive curriculum design for the second year

Martyn Stewart and Clare Milsom

Reflecting on the second year

A number of issues have been raised across the preceding chapters of this book in relation to the academic 'identity' of the second year of study, to the experiences and challenges faced by students in their second year and to shifts in various psychological responses that influence how students engage with their studies in this mid-stage of the course. It is clear from our research and reading of the literature that any phenomenon of a 'sophomore slump', as identified in popular discourse, is complex and multi-faceted. Underperformance evidenced through grade profiles in the second year is recognised for some students and some programmes, but is by no means universal. However, through examination of a mix of measures and indicators, it is clear that a range of factors associated with the second year contribute to increased malaise, confusion, shifts in motivation and growth or a decline in confidence.

Responding to the themes emerging from our research, this chapter summarises the key issues and considers how effective course design may lead to enhanced success at this important pivotal stage of the curriculum. This chapter considers four key themes:

1   Communicating the purpose of the second year;
2   Preparing students for the transition to the second year;
3   Keeping the subject alive;
4   Assessment and feedback for learning.

So what is the second year for? A programme-eye view

The problem?

Quality assurance frameworks characterise the second year in terms of the comprehensive knowledge that students acquire and the development of more critical study approaches. In this sense, the second year may be viewed as a bridging year. Thus, from the perspective of the quality framework, students extend their first-year knowledge and undertake critical analysis as grounding for the final year. Focus group discussions with academic staff, as part of the research project, showed that there was general agreement that, while 'showcase' material may dominate in the first year and the final year was often characterised by the more exciting research specialisms, the second year could be considered more pedestrian in terms of course content:

> the modules on the second year are really kind of core stuff that they have to tick off. (Academic staff)

Models of learning describe the progression of cognitive development from understanding to evaluation. However, as explained in Chapter 2, learning is rarely linear, and complex outcomes can be achieved in the first year through a 'spiral curriculum' concept of repeated reinforcement and application. Curriculum design approaches, then, need to reflect both the connective purpose of the second year and provide students with the opportunity to practise and develop critical and analytical skills. In discussions with staff and students, many described the step up between the first and second years. While some staff felt that they had addressed this challenge, students described a lack of preparedness but perceived this step as a necessary learning experience to prompt a change in study approach:

> I think everyone needs the experience of the jump between first and second year. I think it is an important part of your learning. (Year 2 Student)

Possible solutions?

Without a clear purpose and positive direction, the potential for students to lose their way in the second year is high. Listed below are suggestions to help programme teams present a positive academic identity for the middle years of a programme of study.

- *Programme validation and review:* While most quality assurance processes require critical evaluation of a programme during validation and review the emphasis is on programme and module outcomes. By requiring programme teams to reflect on the outcomes at each level, the academic identity of each year of study could be emphasised. Progression tends to be the single most important factor in determining the 'success', or otherwise, of a level. What tends to happen, though, is that this is usually only considered through a process of exception reporting, where programmes consider the effectiveness of a level only if progression falls below a specified threshold. In modular structures, programme teams could be encouraged to review module appraisal outcomes by level to identify if there are cross-module issues that are specific to level. Programme leaders could be prompted, during a process of annual monitoring, to review the effectiveness of the curriculum in generating the level outcomes as well as the programme and module outcomes. Such a process would then help develop a shared understanding of the characteristics of each level of study. Issues around comprehensiveness and criticality, as identified in the quality assurance frameworks, could be signposted in review documentation requiring academic teams to explicitly discuss how these characteristics are represented in the middle years.

- *Module titles:* Later in this chapter, we provide strategies for 'keeping the subject alive', but before giving these a detailed consideration, it is worth looking simply at the module titles and what they suggest about the academic identity of the middle years. In some programmes, the extension of a module in a subsequent year may be expressed by notation '2', 'II' or 'advanced', defining the middle years with reference to first and final year modules. In order to establish a clear academic identity, modules' titles should be discrete and as indicative of the academic material as possible.

- *Student feedback and representation:* Programme teams should ensure that each level of the programme is supported by a student representative and that there are specific items on Boards of Study agenda that relate to feedback at each level. Programme teams should actively encourage students to discuss issues that extend beyond individual modules or units and relate to the level of study.

Preparing students for the second year

The problem?

A strong theme to emerge from focus group discussions is academic security, which relates to the preparedness of students for their second year. In Chapter 3, it was revealed that developing confidence was a significant theme for students in their first year, and feedback was valued as particularly important in encouraging this. Focus group discussions suggested that for some students the first year did not present any significant level of challenge. Usually, this was a consequence of structured, extended inductions that effectively managed the transition into higher education. Smaller class sizes were often described as significant, aiding socialisation and encouraging students to actively seek support when needed. For other students, initial concerns about coping with academic study at university were alleviated on receipt of decent grades. Some reported getting high grades in their first year that were pleasantly, even unexpectedly, high:

> In one [assignment] I got an 88%. I thought it's really good because it's going to be really good for next year . . . (Year 1 student)

It was evident that many students were entering the second year with a misplaced sense of academic security. This was acknowledged in interviews by both students and academic staff:

I don't think we were prepared enough for the second year because there is a lot more expected of you and you don't realise'. (Year 2 student)

It is almost as though the first year lulls them in to a false sense of security. (Academic Staff)

Similar conclusions have been drawn by researchers elsewhere. Richardson (2004) reported that second-year students had expected workloads in Year 2 to be similar and were surprised by the increase, feeling that, on reflection, the first year had been insufficient as preparation and had created a false sense of security. Scott and Cashmore (2012) similarly describe how students report the significant step up in workload being both unexpected and a cause of angst.

Interviews with academic staff indicated that the academic security of students entering the second year might also be influenced at a curriculum design level by the choices made in selecting curriculum content in the first year. Staff referred to:

the cute fluffy subjects – you know the relatively approachable ones that students like to do in the first year. (Academic staff)

From a curriculum design perspective, it seems evident that there can be some problems in moving from the first year to the second year. As evidenced in Chapters 3 and 4, many students struggled to make the transition successfully, with many reporting confusion, unexpected underperformance, increasingly strategic study strategies, increase in procrastination tendency and/or reduced self-efficacy.

Possible solutions?

Typically, when thinking of academic transitions, we think of induction and usually an 'induction week'. Feedback from students and insights from the literature indicate that we need to think of the transitional phase as being an extended integration between Year 1 and Year 2 rather than a concentrated week of information and activities in the inaugural week of their return.

We can learn much from studies of the first-year transition. Palmer *et al.* (2009) explain how, for new entrants, the transition into university and a new learning culture is not a simple one, but comprises a series of stages. These include a period before students arrive at university, the arrival period and a subsequent settling-in stage which can take weeks or months depending on individuals' success in adaptation. For the purposes of identifying potential interventions to prepare students for their second year, it is useful to think of the Year 2 transition period in similar terms:

- a preparation phase: the latter stages of the first year;
- a bridging phase: the summer break and pre-arrival;
- an incorporation phase: induction activities and settling into the Year 2 study culture.

It is likely that in some programmes and institutions, this approach is already taken. The intention here is to examine an appropriate generalised approach derived from our research findings.

Preparation 1: the first year as preparation for the second year

In Chapter 4, we described how self-regulation and self-efficacy were important to student success in the second year, and results revealed that students on courses that showed a performance 'slump' in the second year reported lower scores for self-efficacy, metacognition and autonomous learning than students on 'non-slumping' courses.

The high-level support, 'cute fluffy subjects' and potential 'spoon-feeding' of the first year, while aiding retention, could be lulling students into a situation of unpreparedness for the next stage. Interestingly, however, some researchers report that on entry to university, students expect to work more independently (Childs and Spencer, 2002). This provides a positive opportunity to develop sequenced activities throughout the first year that progressively let go and foster autonomous learning.

Auditing first-year support

Perhaps the starting point in 'letting go' is to reflect on those points in the first-year curriculum where there is good practice in developing student autonomy and those areas where there is excessive 'hand-holding' that serves to develop a culture of dependency. This might include some auditing activity where the teaching team examine variation in support offered across the first year. Identification factors could cover the following:

- *Teaching methods:* Excessive provision of teaching that fosters passive approaches to study (e.g. lectures).
- *Variation in levels of support:* Between members of the teaching team and between course modules.
- *Ranking tasks/activities that support self-regulation:* It may be possible to allocate various assignments or tasks a rating on the degree to which they support self-regulated learning. This can assist the course team in sequencing these activities appropriately.
- *Feedback:* Examining whether feedback is presented to students in a way that does not undermine confidence and self-efficacy.
- *Feedforward:* Is Year 1 feedback explicitly linked to Year 2 work and are specific actions identified for students to follow up?
- *Reflection and self-assessment:* Where are opportunities provided across the first-year curriculum for students to reflect on their development and is this supporting development of self-regulation in learning?

- *Aligning assessment:* Ensuring forms of assessment in Year 1 are generating skills and attributes that will be utilised in Year 2.

Developing an autonomous learning mind-set

There are many teaching methods that can be used to develop autonomous learning in the first year, including projects or tasks that require students to actively seek out information or support. However, Macaskill and Denovan (2013) point out that developing autonomy is less to do with methods of learning but more concerned with developing capabilities and how students relate to their studies. They examined autonomy from a perspective of positive psychology, in which the focus is placed on identifying character strengths with a view to encouraging further development.

Macaskill and Denovan (2013) describe the deployment of a questionnaire to students on entry in their first year that measured positive psychological variables considered central to development of autonomy. Two weeks later, students were briefed on character strengths for autonomous learning and provided with the personalised reports containing results of their initial test. These results were discussed and rehearsed through group discussion meetings and activities incorporated as part of their electronic personal development portfolio. A further activity involved revisiting their character strengths to reformulate them as part of a curriculum vitae to impress future employers. Assessing the intervention against a control group, the authors found the experiment group to have higher levels of confidence and autonomous learning.

Projects or research

Project work will probably be present throughout the curriculum. Careful consideration of the role of independent research or project work at the tail end of the first year could support developing independent learning skills by providing the opportunity for them to be applied and for the process to be reflected upon. Such a project may well be the culmination of a series of activities or projects designed to progressively develop autonomy and independence. It is important, however, that such activities are appropriately supported, perhaps with less emphasis on summative assessment and with opportunities to observe others' approaches to these tasks and to enable understanding of success factors. According to Bandura (1997), self-efficacy can be enhanced through successfully overcoming a challenge, learning from others' ways of doing things, trying out new things and overcoming anxiety. Without the encouraging context, there runs the risk that anxiety is increased from such tasks and self-efficacy falls.

Opportunities for reflection and consolidation

Students will learn much through their first year. So what have they learned? And how much feedback will students have received by the end of Year 1? What did that feedback conclude? As part of the preparation for Year 2, it would be valuable to provide sufficient opportunity for Year 1 learning to be reflected upon critically. Opportunities for doing this could be multiple and would probably form part of ongoing personal development planning, but it would be useful if experience and learning gained were synthesised in a way valuable to future learning. This could be achieved, for example, by the following:

- Organised critical reflection, where students are encouraged to identify significant steps forward in understanding, thresholds passed, or existing or emerging areas that may need targeted support. Students might also be asked to identify three critical issues in their first year and discuss how they dealt with them and how they might deal with such issues differently if it arose in their second year.
- Synthesising feedback. A tutorial could be set aside in which students are required to collate feedback received on assessed work across the first year with a view to identifying key action points. (This might require some standardisation in feedback provision across the first year.)

Support for workload management

Bearing in mind that a key challenge reported for Year 2 students was the increased workload (Chapter 3) and the finding that Year 2 students were significantly more prone to procrastination (Chapter 4), provision of support to aid students in future self-regulation of workload or time-management may be valuable, either as part of tutorials, extra-curricular support or embedded in Year 1 course delivery. However, in providing such support, it is important that the help or self-help provided does not come across as just another stressor, as, for example, the expectation that students will develop employability skills sometimes does (Chapter 6).

Preparation 2: bridging the first and second years – the summer break

It is not insignificant that for most standard undergraduate degrees, there will be a break of at least four months between the end of the first year, typically in the late spring, and the start of the second year in early autumn. The summer break was specifically highlighted in survey comments as problematic by students. Often, there is little organised academic work over this period, other than, say, recommended reading.

> I felt a little apprehensive after our long summer break . . . I had mixed feelings and was worried whether I did want to continue the degree even though I passed all my modules in the first year. I felt going back I would lack the motivation to work hard after being out of routine over the summer break. (Year 2 student)

The summer break for the third year is similarly long, but in many cases students will be working on dissertation work or at least doing preparatory work towards this, effectively creating some bridge between the years. There are a number of strategies that could be used to create a similar bridge between the first and second year to help in the preparation for the new stage of study and to support development of students' self-regulation.

- *Independent project work:* Selected coursework for Year 2 could be set at the end of the academic year in Year 1 to bridge the summer break and encourage students to work independently. Alternatively, this work may not be part of a summative assessment linked to a specific course module but a cross-modular activity designed to seed interest in key themes that characterise subject content in Year 2. Such a task is more likely to be successful and engage students if the student has a degree of control over the topic selected. Work of this type could be valuable in introducing students to the higher-level learning outcomes expected in Year 2, especially if supported by guidance explaining the step up in expectations.
- *Using social media to maintain contact:* Some programmes utilise social media websites such as Facebook and create programme pages to encourage social interaction among students online. These sites can be valuable for maintaining contact with students over the summer break, either simply to help students and staff keep in touch or more strategically to generate interest in the subject ahead of students arriving in the new semester. However, there are issues around how students see staff involvement in their Facebook communities.
- *Summer newsletters/video reports to inform students of preparatory work:* A newsletter or two could be sent to students over the summer, to maintain contact and introduce news or research relevant to Year 2 study. This might also contain advice from students at higher levels on how best to prepare for the forthcoming year of study.
- *Pre-arrival support:* An information pack could be distributed electronically to students providing information relevant to preparing for Year 2. This might include guidance on characteristics of Year 2 study, standards and expectations. It might include subject-related material or activities to re-ignite subject interest ahead of arrival. It could also include details of the assessment timetable for the year with a task requirement to support workload scheduling.
- *Gaining work experience:* For the following student, being made aware of the need to obtain work experience during their Year 2 induction week (October) appears to have raised anxiety and increased stress:

> Attending the careers session scared me a little! Feel like there is too much experience I need to stand out and meeting people who have not had training contracts until way after graduation has left me worried about my situation when I leave university . . . juggling getting good grades as

well as meeting deadlines for placements and work experience has already become more of a burden than anything else. (Year 2 student)

Alerting students to this at the end of the first year would encourage them to use the long summer break effectively to gain work experience. However, simply telling students that they *should* do so may create stress for some – other incentives, such as university support in making applications or job-hunting at this early stage, or providing an interesting and relevant week-long summer placement as a 'prize' for first-year academic or other achievements could underpin the importance the university places on such experiences.

Preparation 3: Induction in Year 2

In focus group discussions with academic staff and students, second-year induction was frequently described as 'non-existent' or 'rudimentary'. Generally, it was felt that induction was of greatest importance for first-year students (induction is also discussed in Chapter 6). Students felt that the approach often taken by staff when dealing with second-year academic issues was 'you should know this by now', heightening the potential for disengagement among second-year students.

I feel in the second year we are expected to know all this information without anybody telling us. For instance, they will say 'there's a big difference between first and second year essays', but that's all they say. I feel the biggest difference from first year to second year is the lack of anybody to help or ask questions to or just anyone in general. (Year 2 student)

While it is acknowledged that most modules will provide an element of induction, this is often in the context of the course content. A scheduled induction period for second-year students could provide the opportunity to:

- *Welcome students back to the academic department and programme:* Institutional analysis of students' comments in the National Student Survey (Year 3) and mirror surveys (Years 1 and 2) has shown that students identify a shift in focus from the university to the academic department from the first to the second year. Therefore, reinforcing this connection at the departmental level could increase students' engagement with their academic programme of study. This may counter the reduced motivation that some students experience on immediate return to university after the long summer break.
- *Allow students to reflect on their first-year experience:* Where staff and students discussed second-year induction practice, the focus tended to be on course aims and module outcomes. It is suggested that the second-year induction prompts students to reflect on their study approaches and results in order to consider how to improve in the second year.
- *Discuss the expectations of the second year:* While the step up into the second year was acknowledged in staff/student focus groups, it was felt to be implicit

rather than explicit. There was a sense that the complexity of the course content and the workload would increase, but the shift in study approaches required to meet these demands was not explained to students. The single most common regret for second-year students was that they wished they had worked harder to achieve a better grade. Surfacing these issues during induction will enable students to take a proactive role and help identify support if needed to develop effective second-year study strategies.

- *Encourage students to maximise the second year:* We have seen in Chapter 3 that there is a range of external competing pressures for second-year students – for example, it may be the first time they are in rented accommodation, or their social focus may shift from school friends to university friends. Therefore, their singular constant may be their programme of study, but attention towards the programme may not be as strong as it was in their first year. By re-stating the importance of attending, managing deadlines, engaging with the virtual learning environment and using feedback, it may be possible for students to maintain focus on their academic discipline.

Perhaps second-year students would benefit not only from a short, specific induction week but also from a longer transition period, with a range of opportunities to develop the metacognitive processes and strategies across modules as Brooman and Darwent (2013) suggest is effective for first-year students.

Keeping the subject alive: environments that support learning goals

The problem?

In trying to quantify change between the first and second years, one variable that consistently stood out as susceptible to change was motivational focus (Chapter 4), particularly the decline in learning goals. It is probably inevitable that students will focus on obtaining good grades as they progress through their studies, but the decline in the motivation to learn for learning's sake is a matter of concern. Why? Because, as explained in Chapter 4, learning goals are known to be positively associated with learning outcomes and attitudes that are significant at the advanced stages of the undergraduate degree, such as conceptual change learning and favourable acceptance of higher workloads, as well as enjoyment.

> This year though, everything counts towards something. (Year 2 student)

Our evidence indicates that 'the final mark factor' plays an important role, as also found elsewhere (Richardson, 2004). In Chapter 3, we saw from Year 2 focus groups how an increased focus on assessment and performance was more prominent. Students reported adopting strategic, performance-oriented approaches in the second year because their marks are now 'counted' towards the final award classification. In Chapter 4, we reported that knowledge that grades now counted was attributed to increased anxiety and to highly tactical decision-making over the selection of study modules to optimise marks or grades. This selectivity could lead to disengagement with other parts of the course and in part explain the decline in learning goals.

Academic staff interviewed also reported observing these behaviours:

> they [students] become more strategic, they know some more of the rules of the game.

> they [students] are quite jaded actually in the second year. Marks start to count so they start to panic about their work, and the increase in workload.

This might prompt us to question what the desirable study motives *ought to be* during the mid-phase of the undergraduate degree. What do we want the second year to be about? Is the second year too early for this decline in learning to occur? Do we need to do more to keep the subject alive?

Valuable research has been carried out in school classroom settings which shows that learners' personal goal orientations are malleable and influenced, even shaped, by learning environments and teachers' behaviours (Ames, 1992; Anderman and Midgely, 1997; Young, 1997; Kaplan and Maehr, 1999; Wolters, 2004). For example, where the goal structure of the classroom setting was perceived to be learning-oriented, learners are more inclined to adopt personal mastery goals. More recently, Daniels *et al.* (2013) attributed some effect to the prevailing climate surrounding teaching. Their study compared the personal goal orientations of new teachers and found that teachers in secondary school, where cultures of testing and competition are well established, were more likely to implement performance classroom goals despite initial learning goal intentions.

This might prompt us to reflect on whether prevailing cultures of performativity in higher education are influencing how teachers act, and on the cues and signals we communicate to students about what is valued. The following quotation is from a Year 2 student in response to a question on how to improve second-year induction:

> If they can think of something you are going to be learning as well – as opposed to saying 'this is going to be an exam; that is going to have an exam' . . .

Possible solutions?

Snyder (1971) and Ramsden (1992) pointed to the existence of two curricular 'worlds' – a manifest one defined by the written curriculum and intended learning outcomes, and a 'hidden curriculum', defined by students in terms of what was necessary to appease teachers and achieve success. If we accept that students will take their cues about what is important and valued from the language, practices and activities they encounter, it follows that we need to reflect our priorities through our own messages and practice.

- *Awareness of the goal structures promoted:* There are many cues that can influence how students come to perceive performance or learning to be important. A simple example might be the way a lecturer responds to low attendance by motivating students: 'remember to turn up as this year counts toward your degree'. Drip feeding of such messages, where not balanced by emphasis on wider learning, can reinforce orientation towards performance goals. It may be that particular effort is required in the second year to mitigate the effects of a natural lean towards assessment focus, through language and encouragement that emphasises subject mastery to achieving learning outcomes. Acknowledging that assessment is a powerful cue for student learning, particular attention could be paid to assessment designs that emphasise learning gains.
- *Keeping the subject alive:* How we 'market' subject learning in Year 2 may be influential. In recruiting students to university, our marketing literature and discussions at open days will typically, and quite appropriately, focus on the learning that students will gain – the excitement of a new subject; even the chance to live that dream. Do we promote the learning in the second year in a similar way? Possibly not. Placing more attention on how we keep a passion for the subject alive in Year 2 and enthuse students towards the upcoming academic content of the second year can send positive signals that support mastery goals.
- *Providing choice:* Provision of choice is well recognised in increasing learners' intrinsic motivation in a subject and sense of autonomy and control (Deci and Ryan, 1985; Cordova and Lepper, 1996). Studies have shown how students who feel they have more personal control over their learning and behaviour are more likely to do well (Pintrich and Schunk, 2002). Choice may be provided in many ways, through optional modules, study pathways within core modules and the freedom to choose topics of interest in assessment designs. Inclusion of project or enquiry-based learning designs also support students' development towards autonomy. Ciani *et al.* (2011) suggest that support for autonomous learning from teachers can act as a buffer against the decline of learning goals.

Assessment, marking and feedback: considerations for the second year

It's been good, it's been really good, there's been lots more work. It's like they have missed out a step almost between first year and second year . . . (Year 2 student)

The problem?

We have already seen that students' perceptions of what is important in the second year can stem in part from the cues encountered in the learning environment: the 'hidden curriculum' as determined by the messages and attention weighted to various elements of the curriculum. As one lecturer explained, 'the first year marks don't count and you only have to get 40%. We are not demanding very much really'. But by the second year, the marks do 'count'. While the extent to which the second-year marks count varies across the sector (Yorke, 2008), the potential finality of these marks has a significant impact on the importance that students place on second-year summative assessment.

Perceptions of the importance of assessment were not only found to shift for students, however. It was also felt that academic staff also approached the curriculum differently. Compounding the increased workload and challenge staff also, almost uniformly, felt that they became tougher markers in the second year in response to the 'final mark factor'. This increase in marking severity contrasted with potentially more lenient, permissive first-year marking practices that were designed to encourage students and increase their academic confidence – which may also contribute to the false sense of academic security discussed in the previous section.

> I will mark them more harshly in second year than the first year so perhaps their grades are a reflection of our expectations
>
> If anything we mark harder definitely
>
> There's definitely not the flattering
>
> It isn't the ego boosting marks they have had previously. (Academic staff comments)

Potential solutions

There are a number of implications here that specifically relate to assessment design and assessment criteria.

- *Assessment for learning:* The assessment procedures are probably the strongest influence on how students approach their learning (Ramsden, 1992). Church *et al.* (2001) suggest that students can be encouraged to deviate away from mastery goals where a heavy emphasis is placed on evaluating learning. It is useful to distinguish between assessment that has a primary purpose to measure learning and assessment strategies that direct and control student learning based on the power of summative assessment (Gibbs and Simpson, 2005; Carless, 2007). In a review, McDowell *et al.* (2011) explain how assessment designs and environments that are primarily focused on supporting learning will tend to be rich in feedback and dialogue (formal and informal), include tasks that are authentic and provide opportunities to practise and apply learning, and help develop independence and autonomy.

Assessment in the second year can, therefore, play an important role in promoting a broader 'learning culture' (Sadler, 1998). In this sense, the purpose and relevance of the assessment task are deemed critical if assessment is to be valued in promoting learning goals. This might require careful consideration of how assessment designs in Year 2 build upon Year 1 and form part of the preparation for future study in a clear and explicit way. Crisp (2011) proposes the term 'integrative assessment' for tasks that are primarily focused on influencing students' approaches to future learning and that have a strong emphasis on developing self-evaluation, integrating past feedback and developing metacognitive abilities. As part of the whole-curriculum assessment strategy, such integrative assessment designs can play an important role in extending students' developing autonomy throughout the middle stage of their course.

- *Familiarisation with Level 5 (second-year) standards:* Work with students early in the semester to show how module learning outcomes will be assessed and the criteria that will be applied to evaluate student work. Discuss with students the differences between the criteria used in the second and the first year and develop activities that require second-year students to actively engage with the criteria. For example, using criteria, ask students to identify the key 'attributes' of second-year work, provide examples of second-year work and ask students to mark it and discuss their marks with each other. Early formative peer assessment will also ensure that students engage with the assessment criteria in a 'safe', meaningful, way that will increase their understanding of the academic standards of the second year.
- *Parity in understanding of 'Level 5 (second-year) standards':* Course teams and markers need to communicate and develop a shared understanding of the academic standards associated with Level 5. With second-year marks contributing to the final award, there is more emphasis on internal and external moderation, but this often takes place at the end of the module. Early discussions around expectations, 'levelness' and marking approaches will assist a collective understanding of the academic standards and requirements of the second year that can be communicated to students not only through more formal assessment tasks but also in informal discussions around expectations of this year of study.

From step-change to smooth progression

At a conceptual level, we might see an idealised spiral curriculum model, in which learners' existing understandings and skills in, say, knowledge, autonomy and critical thinking are harnessed in the first year, developed progressively in a continuum through the second year and reach their optimum development and application in the final year. But in reality, the curriculum will be a fragmented collage, with many factors, structural and perceptual, that will militate against this – the compartmentalisation of skills and cognitive outcomes associated with academic level, a timetable that presents intense periods of study followed by long breaks of study silence, and then, of course, those value-messages that intentionally or inadvertently direct students to parts of the course that 'matter', influencing study behaviours along the way. The challenge for the curriculum designer is to smooth these transitions between the levels, and in doing so to recognise the important role of the second year in maximising student success.

Chapter 6

Implications for student support

Elena Zaitseva, Sue Darwent and Sue Thompson

'Lost in transition?'

Historically, the research literature on the student experience has focused on the first year, seen as important from the perspective of student adaption, retention and progression (McInnis, 2001; Rickinson and Rutherford, 1995; Terenzini *et al.* 1994; Whittaker, 2008). This focus on the first-year experience has been reflected in major national and institutional initiatives, both in the UK and internationally, aimed at enhancing students' transition and retention, for example, the Scottish Quality Enhancement Theme for 2005 on First Year: Engagement and Empowerment,[1] and similar work in Australia (James *et al.*, 2010) and the USA (National Resource Center for The First-Year Experience and Students in Transition in the USA).[2]

In recent years, UK research on the student experience has had a particular focus on student transition – into, through and out of higher education, generated by the widening participation in higher education agenda. The Higher Education Funding Council for England (HEFCE), in its guide to good practice for widening participation strategies, articulated a life-cycle model of student support covering aspiration raising, pre-entry, admission, first term/semester, moving through the course and progression into employment and/or postgraduate study (HEFCE, 2001). Support for student transition has been the focus of much institutional work and of a national programme (What Works? Student Retention and Success 2008–2011: see Thomas, 2012).

This emphasis on student transition into the university and the first-year experience has resulted in readily accessible resources and extensive academic and pastoral support for first-year students. This is not always the case for second-year students who consistently demonstrate lower level of satisfaction than other years with the support they receive. This was found to be the case in our project and reflected elsewhere (e.g. Horton *et al.* 2013). While transition initiatives might acknowledge difficulties students face when moving into the second year, they do not necessarily directly address them by developing specific actions or interventions related to student support. Institutional projects aimed at enhancing second-year support are more common in the USA – see, for example, a major institutional project at Belmont University[3] and the initiatives mentioned in Chapter 1. Only a handful of such initiatives are found in the UK – for example, Second Year Blues at the University of Huddersfield[4] and Second Year Mathematics BeyOnd Lectures (SYMBoL) at Loughborough University, a project aimed at enhancing the second-year experience of undergraduate mathematicians.[5]

Previous chapters have reflected on some particular and different challenges that the second year presents. These challenges have direct implications for student support. As seen in Chapter 4, second-year students can exhibit various signs of 'self-regulatory failure', such as a drop in motivation, a tendency to procrastinate, academic anxiety and a higher level of general stress that can affect their academic performance. American research echoes our project findings; for example, Lemons and Richmond (1987), as cited in Hunter *et al.* (2010), describe the sophomore slump as 'a period of developmental confusion, that results from a student's struggle with competence, desiring autonomy, establishing identity and developing purpose' (Hunter *et al.* 2010: 38). While many second-year students appeared to be 'in search of their own definition of success . . . ' (ibid.), our research has shown that not all of them are approaching this search with confidence or knowledge of how to achieve success. This has direct implications for learner support – its timeliness, continuity and relevance. A steep step up between the first and second years in relation to a new set of academic skills, curriculum demands and time on task, explored in Chapters 2 and 5, raises questions about how students can be helped to successfully negotiate this new stage in their development as learners.

This chapter explores project findings related to learner support in the second year, as perceived by staff and students. Specifically, it covers two areas of support: academic or study support which assist students in refining and strengthening their academic skills, and family and peer support. Although counselling and well-being support (pastoral care for second-year students provided by professional services) were not explicitly researched as part of the project, implications for these services, where identified, are also discussed.

Based on predominantly qualitative data collected through focus groups and interviews with staff and students from various academic programmes and utilising, where possible, outcomes of smaller initiatives within faculties and other institutional datasets, this chapter explores the following questions:

- What are second-year students' needs for academic and pastoral support?
- What support structures are available and how do second-year students access this support?
- Are there specific time-points when this support could be critical for second-year students' academic engagement and progression?

The evidence from this institutional research is discussed in relation to the literature, and some recommendations are made for consideration when planning future student support.

Academic/study support

Perceived needs

Wider research demonstrates that pre-university experience plays an important role in how students approach their academic work and in their expectations of support (Bowles *et al.* 2011; Miller, 2005; Richardson, 2003; Thomas, 2011; Thomas, 2012). In our study, younger students who came to university directly from school described being heavily coached and given regular, extensive feedback which left them ill-prepared for the independent learning expected at university. In many cases, greater support in the first year of their course, within modules or from personal tutors, appears to have paid insufficient attention to preparing students for the transition to the more demanding second year. Some mature students commented on too much support or 'spoon feeding' in the first year which is, as a nursing student observed, 'not helping to cut the umbilical cord' and allow for the independent development of a learner.

The long summer break between the first and the second years generated anxiety for many students. They believed that loss of contact with the university for more than four months contributed to diminished motivation and to worry about losing knowledge and skills gained in the first year. Some students articulated a need for continuity of communication and academic support through planning and goal-setting following their first-year exams. For example, one student commented,

> . . . You've done your [first] year, bye, we'll contact you in August . . . I don't think there was any . . . 'let's meet up at the end, a few weeks before the end [of the first year]. This is what you are expecting next year, this is what your priorities should be over the summer, maybe you should do this . . . ' I think that would have been very helpful to say what my direction is.

As discussed in Chapter 5, in returning to the university in Year 2, students found induction to be either 'non-existent' or 'rudimentary'. The overall feeling was that induction of the second-year cohort was a low priority with students picking up a 'you should have known everything by now' perspective from staff. It seems that 'slumping' students – those who experienced a drop in performance and engagement – were in particular need of help with setting goals, explanation of new workload and 'modelling' consequences of losing/dropping marks in the second year.

When final-year students were asked to reflect retrospectively on their second year, many discussed their struggle with the step up in difficulty of their course, particularly on technical modules, and this is where they would have welcomed support and guidance:

> . . . it's like they [academics] have missed out a step almost between first year and second year. It's like going from step 3 to step 5 just in the amount

of work and the level of understanding required . . . It's not easy to figure it out yourself, you need to ask your tutors, to talk about that . . .

Staff noticed that those students who were not able to adapt to changing requirements and demands, failed second-year exams and decided to leave were most likely to have a deeper underlying problem which had originated earlier but not been shared with a personal or academic tutor. The challenge for teaching staff is to identify whether students are experiencing genuine difficulties and need urgent support or whether the behavioural patterns are a temporary reaction to challenges of the 'middle year' from which students will recover.

Help with making module choices was seen as important. Students who by the end of the first year had only a vague idea of modules they wanted to take, and who were not supported in identifying the most suitable route for them, chose their optional modules based either on advice of other students or often at random, rather than through discussion or advice from a member of staff. A student-interviewee explained,

> I think I had a panic as well, I thought 'I don't know how to choose the modules, I don't know what I'm choosing' . . . I ended up choosing by asking other people what they were doing.

These decisions contributed to disengagement and poor performance, as in Paul's story. One student noted that the second year was 'a bit like a trial and error year . . . ' in relation to module choices, while another one found that choosing options 'strategically' was not always beneficial:

> In my second year . . . I dropped the subjects I maybe liked but I wasn't always good at – to take subjects I hadn't studied before. I'd find I didn't like them and wouldn't really work that hard . . .

The following case study (Figure 6.1) describes student experiences of starting their second year.

Provision of, and access to, learner support

A range of second-year needs were specified by the students and also acknowledged by the staff who were interviewed. Project research demonstrated that various factors impacted on both support provision and students' willingness to access it.

Most staff interviewed in the focus groups believed that individual tutor support (academic or personal) was available to second-year students but recognised that there was often lack of continuity in relation to that:

> . . . Students get used to [regular personal tutor sessions] and then, in the second year . . . they are not timetabled. So we've gone from 'you might see

Methodology: Ten second-year Law student volunteers recorded their thoughts about their academic experience on digital voice recorders as they progressed through the first four weeks of the semester. Data collection was based on Critical Incident Technique originated by Flanagan (1954). As soon as possible after an event that participants perceived as notable, significant or meaningful, they recorded their responses. Students responded to a prompt list which was provided to ensure that they gave sufficient detail for the incident to be analysed. The recordings were downloaded each week, transcribed and then analysed using general thematic analysis.

Experiences of starting second year

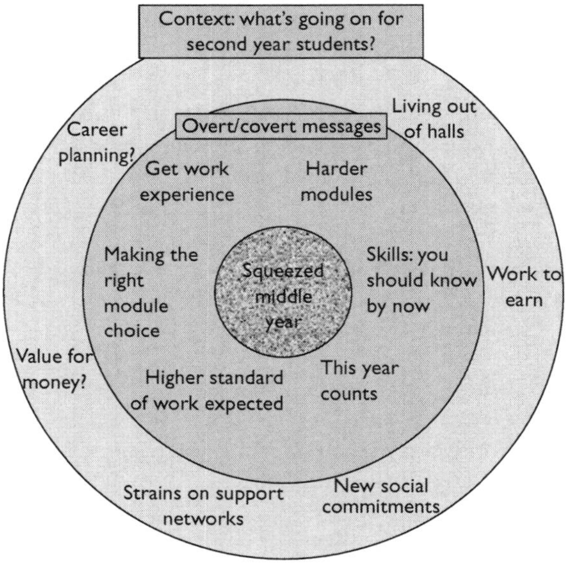

- Context: what's going on for second year students?
- Overt/covert messages
- Career planning?
- Living out of halls
- Get work experience
- Harder modules
- Making the right module choice
- Squeezed middle year
- Skills: you should know by now
- Work to earn
- Value for money?
- Higher standard of work expected
- This year counts
- Strains on support networks
- New social commitments

Main findings: On returning to university students immediately felt under pressure from both overt and covert messages given over the two-day induction (much shorter than the week-long event for first-year students) and during modules. Not only were students made aware that course content would be harder, but higher standards and criticality would be rewarded. At the same time, they were encouraged, and given support, to apply for work experience and training contracts, and to develop their CVs. Several noted that courses began swiftly, with coursework deadlines given immediately, while at the same time, changing circumstances external to the course were not taken into account, e.g. reforming friendship groups, living independently for the first time, financial worries. These internal and external pressures led to some considering whether they still felt motivated to continue and whether the course gave value for money. Although they found the first few weeks challenging, all ten adapted to the increased demands and continued with their studies.

"I can definitely see the difference between beginning a module in first year and beginning one in second year as there was no room for being gently introduced; we were thrown in at the deep end which provided a bit of a shock to the system after such a long summer break. Getting back into the habit of studying and motivating myself to study has, admittedly, taken a while." (Student M, at the end of the first week).

Figure 6.1 Experiences of starting the second year

your tutor every two weeks' to possibly never at all, to every week in the third year and it just ruins it all . . . It just seems like we have set up a structure that just forgets about the middle . . .

Staff acknowledged that the pressure to perform well in the National Student Survey (NSS), where the results influence league table position of the institution, leads to Year 3 teaching and support becoming a priority for programme teams. Experienced and enthusiastic staff who can 'excite and inspire' are given third-year modules to teach and dissertations to supervise. Second-year students are perceived as being more knowledgeable and skilled than first-year students. This, together with high student-to-staff ratios, encourages staff to focus on 'needier' groups:

> The problem is you've got . . . a high staff-student ratio. Focus of your attention is only going to be on certain students – the ones taking your attention are the ones doing dissertations or the ones just starting university, so if it's like that it's always going to be an issue . . .

Many academics interviewed agreed that second-year students themselves should generally be more active in searching for the resources they need and in making use of them or should be actively prompted to do so. One of the students commented on 'discovering' Study Skills workshops provided by Student Services:

> Induction was very good because it gave lots of information, for example, the study skills workshop. It tied in very nicely after talking about the 'sophomore slump' as it was telling the benefits of going to the workshops. I feel that before, when the information about the study skills workshop was just on email, the importance didn't come across. This could be down to the fact that the emails are sent to everyone and not personal so I didn't tend to pay much attention whereas in the induction I knew whatever was said was important.

This indicates that the way in which information is given, or services are marketed, may impact on take-up and highlights the importance of paying attention to the effectiveness, or otherwise, of communication systems.

Induction

Chapter 5 indicated that dedicated second-year induction is a prerequisite of successful transition. Students in our study believed that induction could play a beneficial role in helping them focus and avoid slumping:

> Maybe something could be done online as an induction into second year. New study techniques and how to get a head start in that second year because it does now actually mean something . . .

> I think if they showed me [at induction] some correlation graph or something, you know – the relationship between studying for this many hours and getting this result. I don't think students necessarily understand the 25 per cent [weighting of second-year marks in the degree classification] and how that works, how it breaks down . . .

However, care is needed in deciding what information should be included and how it is communicated at the beginning of the semester, as students can have diverse responses. In the second-year Law School induction, information was given about the sophomore slump and graphs showed how previous students whose marks did not dip in the second year tended to achieve better final degree awards. While this motivated some students, others responded with raised anxiety:

> Although the 'sophomore slump' may be on a national scale, I personally felt it was unnecessary and counterproductive to scare students. I felt positive encouragement is more effective than negative but this may have just been how I felt rather than the majority opinion. I think it would have been more effective to slowly and gently in each module's introduction lectures emphasize the academic step up so that way the message would be received, but done in a less dramatic way.

Personal tutoring

Students who took part in the research commented that personal tutoring in the second year and academic support in general were limited and did not always meet their needs. While in the first-year tutorial time was likely to be embedded in the timetable, in the second year it was more likely to be an option with students being told to 'find your tutor and contact him/her if you need to'. When personal tutor support was in place and fully utilised, students commented that these contacts were essential to their academic progression and general well-being. Those who did not have regular contact with a personal tutor missed not only study-related help, but also psychological support and guidance:

> Would be good [to have more personal tutoring] throughout the year as well as the reflective opportunities . . . Not just in terms of discipline but in terms of 'where are you now and what next and how does it fit within the framework of being a student?'

Experiencing difficulties in contacting their personal tutor appeared to contribute to feelings of academic isolation and led to more serious or unresolved problems. Student Union Advice Centre statistics analysed as part of the project indicated that second-year students' concerns with academic progress often resulted in formal complaints – these were problems not picked up or resolved by personal tutors.

Dedicated tutorial support, providing continuity of support through the initial two years of study in particular, was perceived as important by current and former students. One of the alumni commented,

> . . . They never set meetings up or anything like that with our personal tutors . . . As I said, second year there was no contact. I think we had half an hour at the start of the year when we first went in, when they were just introducing themselves. But we didn't get an email or anything after that, no contact details – [that's why I got lost].

The importance of regular contact in identifying students at risk was often mentioned by those students experiencing a noticeable drop in performance in their second year:

> Having a contact once a semester is absolute minimum, I think . . . That would have made all the difference to me . . . [Personal tutor] could have looked at my marks half way through my second year . . . Look you are failing, the marks are really not, you know, they are not up to scratch. I could have turned that around the second half of the second year . . .

At the same time, evidence collected in the study of May and Bousted (2004), as well as in our project, reveals that giving access to support by putting the onus on students to approach their tutors at set times does not necessarily result in those who most need support getting it. Some students 'understandably felt intimidated about taking up what they saw as the valuable time of tutors, especially when the tutor proved difficult to access' (May and Bousted, 2004: 44).

Social support

Peer support, study groups and peer mentoring

Students noted that one of the factors that promoted engagement in the second year was peer support, including peer learning groups. These were often established informally during the pre-university access programme, or in the first year, and remained active through the second year of study. As one of the students from an Engineering course explained,

> Our [peer] group usually gets together after our classes instead of going home . . . Others . . . join us from time to time, some stay longer, some don't stay at all. We usually stay till around half seven, half eight, depending what time we get kicked out of the room, get our coursework done, get our maths classes done, so it's not as stressful . . . It is quite a big group – if one of us doesn't know the problem somebody will know . . .

The group was formed from a 'core' of people who knew each other from an earlier 'access' programme and who experienced a need to talk to somebody about lecture materials, practicals or a particular problematic coursework. Although the group was open to everybody on the course, a good work ethic and willingness to put regular effort into learning were the main criteria for acceptance. Another peer learning group formed in the first year from a group of friends who 'are all generally proactive' and again work ethic seemed to play an important role in inclusion. For both groups peer support was instrumental in retention, as all students participating in the group successfully passed their first year and demonstrated good results in the second year.

Learning Resource Centre staff noted that self-formed study groups become more visible in the second year:

> They . . . form their own study groups in the second year, they are a bit more confident whatever it is. We do see them coming in together, making much more use of the booking facilities and planning their study. They are very motivated to plan in advance, so the more service we can provide with bookings and so on. So I think there is a kind of focus on even doing things in an efficient way maybe that there's not been in first year . . .

Academic staff noticed that the new peer groups formed in Year 2 were different from those students might have formed in Year 1, reflecting their performance aims (students who would like to do better and enhance their performance would pair up with more academically able students) and type of support they require:

> Quite often it's in Year 2 when you'll find these little hybrid age groups . . . In Year 2 it seems to be more performance or expectation specified, and then it's often those groups that actually survive into Year 3 . . .

It was also found that peer support groups arose organically out of tutor groups or friendship groups, or from officially established relationships such as mentoring or poster project groups that originated in the first year. Anecdotally, staff noticed that many Year 2 and Year 3 students have friends whose last names begin with the same letter, due to the alphabetical allocation of first-year tutor groups.

Problems can occur when groups or relationships are disrupted. For example, one student restarted her second year after a period of illness and then felt isolated as her previous friendship group had moved on and she did not know anyone from the year group she joined. This happened with Paul (see opening story) when his friend left the university after the first year and he felt socially isolated. This is a reminder that staff cannot assume that students are settled into their friendship groups and course because they have completed one year.

Peer influence was mentioned on other occasions: if students are working hard, their peers tend to follow. There is also evidence to the contrary, as friends or roommates can become disengaged and influence each other. This may start in the first year and subsequently have an impact on the student's second-year performance. As one student who experienced a profound 'slump' in the second year described,

> We just talked all day and socialised and stuff [with roommates] . . . It was great really, we had a great laugh, we could entertain each other all day . . . Some days I would be really constructive, go to the library and stay in there for half the day, I have always used the libraries . . . then some days would be less constructive, to say the least . . .
>
> Two of my roommates left university after the first year, it was difficult for me to stay afloat . . .

Similar conclusions have been drawn by researchers elsewhere. Tinto (1997) found that learning communities (such as students who learn together in groups and create a network of people that they feel attached to) provide support and help, to deepen learning as discussion about the course material takes place, both in and out of the classroom. It has long been recognised that social support groups act as a buffer against the onset of anxiety and depression during periods of stress and in enhancing self-esteem (Wilcox, 1981). It is also known that the establishment of cooperative learning groups or supportive learning communities accelerates the study process in both traditional and online learning environments (Marjanovic, 1999; Slavin, 1996), and enhances psychological well-being in undergraduates by developing a sense of purpose and identity. Peer learning groups help not only in general adaptation to university life but also through enlarging the Zone of Proximal Development (ZPD) of both mature and young students (Vygotsky, 1978). Vygotsky defined ZPD as a distance 'between the actual developmental level as determined by independent problem solving and the level of potential development as determined through problem solving . . . in collaboration with more capable peers' (ibid., p. 86). Second-year students, more than students at other levels, find that their peers are instrumental in helping them to reach a better level of understanding in a stress-free, friendly environment (e.g. without the involvement of academic or support staff).

Peer mentoring is another valued support mechanism. Those students who went through a slump and managed to get back on track commented on several occasions that being warned about slump or helped by a senior student-mentor who experienced it could have benefitted them. As one of the final-year interviewees commented,

> if somebody came in [when I was starting my second year] and said 'I'm a third year student now I didn't [work hard] in my second year . . . '. If you had those opportunities to ask questions and learn from other people's mistakes . . .

When leaders of the Students' Union were interviewed, they mentioned that in faculties that run peer mentoring schemes, students are much more 'self-sufficient' and less reliant on the Union's support in student engagement. Some second-year mentors for first-year students (as part of faculty-led initiatives and funded projects) noticed that supporting others helped them to reflect on their own learning experience and what was missing from it, and helped students feel good about progress they were making as learners:

> [Mentoring] helped me realise how much I have learnt, made me feel very mature . . .

Some other benefits of mentoring for both first- and second-year students are mentioned in the case study below (Box 6.1)

Family support

The project findings indicated that the second year is a period where many students experience motivational and goal-setting difficulties which often manifest themselves in underperformance and withdrawal – 'partial' (e.g. low attendance, strategic attitude to their learning) or 'actual' (e.g. considering leaving or leaving university).

Box 6.1   Mentoring in the school of law: Case study

Mentoring has been an invaluable part of the first-year experience of Law students for a number of years, and various approaches have been taken. Initially, the course leader simply asked second- and third-year students to volunteer to mentor new students, and they carried out this task with some informal training and tutor support. The support given was highly valued:

> I would just like to say that the mentor appointed to me has been great. I found that just putting my ideas to her and receiving feedback has been more than reassuring to me. It made me feel more confident about how I was tackling problem questions and when I was on the right lines in essays. A great help and I have recommended it to others. A great source of support in finding my feet as well, as I do lack self confidence and I have found that having [mentor] there when in doubt has been a huge support.

In focus group discussions, mentors also listed many benefits, including increased confidence, developing communication skills, seeing how far they themselves have progressed, being organised and seeing another person's perspective, as well as increased motivation and preparing for work:

> Mentoring the Year 1 students made me eager to get back into studying as early as possible. Explaining the university process to new students made me realise how simplistic it all works but how you do not know what to expect.

> Having a similar mentoring relationship in a work experience situation means that I have experienced mentoring from both sides. This will help when I become a solicitor and have a trainee working with me.

However, there were a number of problems – for example, mentees not turning up, communication difficulties at the beginning of the year and mentors unsure about how far they should help. As a result, a short training programme was devised, run by a member of the university volunteering group. The scheme continued to run successfully. One student, however, noted conflicting feelings, in that he was keen to use his experiences to help new students, but did not want to inadvertently become an agent of the institution, which training seemed to him to imply. In response, a short online training scheme was established to raise awareness of potential issues such as collusion, plagiarism and personal safety, as well as outlining the responsibilities and limitations of mentoring relationships. This could be completed in mentors' own time. The mentoring programme was extended through an e-mentoring trial scheme to students pre-arrival (not successfully, because of a low level of uptake), and some second-year students have requested similar help:

> I feel like it would be helpful to have a mentor or just someone to ask questions to – for example, knowing how to use journals or how to change how we write our essays. I feel in second year we are totally left on our own and expected to know all this information but without anybody telling us. For instance they will say 'there's a big difference between first and second year essays', but that's all they say. I feel the biggest difference from first year to second year is the lack of not even support just the lack of anybody to help or ask questions to or just anyone in general.

Recently, third and fourth years have developed student-led online support for specific modules on Facebook.

What we also found is that many slumpers are 'silent sufferers', not necessarily sharing their problems with personal tutors or student support services until it is too late. A study by Darwent (2011) determined that a large percentage of first-year students cite their mother as the person they would most turn to in times of difficulty, followed by other family members or partners. Only 0.5 per cent of the total group would choose to go to a professional advisor (Figure 6.2).

Similarly, family is often the main source of support and encouragement when students are making decisions about leaving or staying after the second year, as in the following case:

Interviewer: So what made you stay?
Respondent: The family. The support from my family and my friends and my partner . . . My mum was so stressed out . . . She knew I would be making a decision based on a few months as opposed to the rest of my life kind of thing. I got lots of support from them . . .

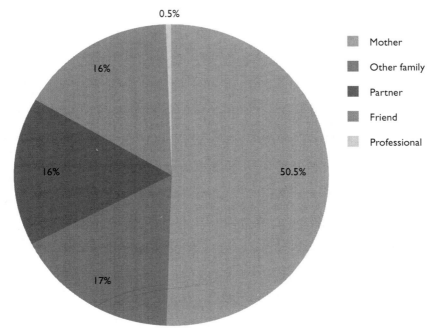

Figure 6.2 Who would you turn to in difficulty?

Interviewer: Did you try to go and talk to student support and counselling services?
Respondent: No I didn't, because it's a bit . . . it's a great service, but I would find
              it nerve wracking going in . . . I find it a bit . . . mentally weak.

These feelings were echoed by another interviewee in giving the example of his
mother taking on the role of academic advisor and personal tutor:

> I guess . . . seeing the bad marks that made me quite anxious, I even had thought
> of dropping out of uni. It was my mum [who helped me] . . . She just sort of
> said: why give up now, choose what you want to do for your dissertation . . .

A lack of willingness to take up help from university student services was a
recurrent topic in interviews with 'slumpers', particularly among male students:

> I didn't use anything like that [student counselling or student welfare
> services], if anything I would feel apprehensive to go there because I would
> feel that maybe I wasn't at the right place . . . I sort of felt that welfare was
> more for disabled people, less privileged people . . .
>
> But now I think they might have helped me get back on track, maybe with
> their help I could have done it faster . . .

The research demonstrated that encouragement from friends and family can have a significant effect upon academic integration, commitment to the institution and decisions to persist with the course (Cabrera *et al.,* 1993).

Challenges of second-year support

The second year is a pivotal stage in the student life cycle, and academic and professional support staff need to be sensitive to a complex range of issues that students may face in this important year. As the literature demonstrates, students' attitude towards the institution and the process of learning is adversely affected by a lack of care and support (White *et al.,* 1999).

There are some direct implications of the project findings for academic support and student well-being. Understanding the challenges of this stage in the student life cycle and being able to identify students in genuine need of support is important. While some students who show indications of 'slump' might easily recover and achieve in the final year, others might need more attention and support. A second-year 'slump' can lead to missed opportunities, a lack of belief in one's own abilities and sometimes to a student leaving the course or university. This is particularly important as more students now commence university study from diverse academic backgrounds and levels of preparation (McInnis, 2001; Thomas, 2012).

Our research has highlighted the importance of purposeful and concise *induction*, welcoming students into their second year, allaying concerns and encouraging realistic expectations. In a study of first-year transition, Brooman and Darwent (2013) found that the initial induction provided opportunities for social integration and developing a feeling of belonging, while a longer transition period enabled students to develop other factors associated with success, such as self-efficacy. As with a spiral curriculum (Chapter 2), perhaps a spiral induction and transition period would be beneficial (Maguire, 2006): revisiting similar topics in subsequent years, but in increasingly challenging ways, for example, discussing 'good' and 'poor' excerpts from past students' anonymised essays in first-year tutor group sessions, while in the second year, students could bring in their own previously submitted essays and decide together how they would mark them, according to given criteria.

The blurring of the boundaries between the professional and academic spheres has been highlighted as an important 'Third Space' (Whitchurch, 2008) in higher education. This linking of the professional and academic spheres can be seen in the recent work of the Higher Education Academy in student engagement and success. The key findings from the 'What Works? Student Retention and Success' project show the importance of students having a strong sense of belonging in higher education which is the result of engagement, and that this is most effectively nurtured through mainstream activities (Thomas, 2012).

Personal tutors oversee academic development and are often the 'first port of call' for all student concerns, advising on issues that fall under a professional remit and signposting to other sources of support where appropriate (Lindsay, 2011).

Our findings are consistent with wider research on the importance of personal tutoring and its potential to enhance the student experience, achievement and retention (Laycock, 2009; Robbins, 2006; Thomas, 2012; Thomas and Hixenbaugh, 2006; Yorke and Longden, 2008). The widening participation agenda in the UK and greater student diversity have increased the breadth of student needs, resulting in personal tutors feeling overstretched and out of their depth (Lindsay, 2011; Thomas and Hixenbaugh, 2006). Neville (2007) explored the challenges experienced by students in relation to personal tutoring and found that being unable to access help and advice from their personal tutors when they required it was the primary concern. Our research showed this to be a particular problem for our second-year students.

The need for improved and consistent personal tutoring provision throughout the three years of the typical UK degree is not a straightforward institutional task (limited resources and other constraints related to the staff–student ratio have been noted in this and other chapters). It is important that university-wide policies acknowledge the need for local ownership and implementation, allowing for discipline-based tailoring. It would seem important that personal tutoring is given a high priority, with training and support provided to help tutors to be fully effective in their role.

Developing *social learning* approaches, promoting group work and setting targets for the year could be key priorities for the second year. Actively fostering the establishment of supportive peer groups could benefit second-year students as this is associated with reduced personal problems such as anxiety, depression and loneliness, and also enhanced academic performance and university experience in general (Peat *et al.,* 2001). Providing opportunities for, and encouraging the formation of, self-support networks (student mentors, study groups) could be useful interventions. However, in the light of the Law School experience, it should be noted that staff appearing to 'take over' an aspect of support that students feel competent to carry out may result in antagonism. Peer mentoring (third-year students mentoring second-year students) could be encouraged where possible as part of the curriculum, and student innovations, such as Facebook support sites, could be constructively supported from a distance.

A considerable proportion of second-year students who do not withdraw but complete their studies may, nevertheless, have underperformed because of disengagement from the educational and social processes of university life. Second-year student support can shift the focus from the issue of student marks and retention to one of supporting the engagement and empowerment of all students. Success 'will be measured not simply in terms of whether students continue on their programmes but whether, in doing so, they are provided with the opportunity to achieve their full potential' (Whittaker, 2008: 4).

Notes

1 See http://www.enhancementthemes.ac.uk/enhancement-themes/completed-enhance
   ment-themes/first-year
2 See http://www.sc.edu/fye/
3 See http://forum.belmont.edu/news/2011/08/22/sophomore-year-experience-
   launches-with-center-summit/
4 See http://www.hud.ac.uk/tali/projects/tl_projects_13/second%20year%20blues/
5 See http://sym.lboro.ac.uk/

Chapter 7

Maximising the use of institutional data

Mantz Yorke, Peter Hoekstra and Wayne Turnbull

Data-rich institutions

Institutions possess a large amount of data bearing on 'the student experience'. The data are likely to be dispersed in various parts of the institution, and hence different interested parties may have access to only a partial picture. The study on which this book is based unearthed a number of data sources, many of which were held in local repositories rather than in an institutional repository. The concept of the institutional 'data warehouse', exemplified in the case study from the University of Amsterdam (UvA) later in this chapter, has obvious attraction. Various contributions to the European First Year Experience Conference in 2014 (particularly a keynote presentation from Mark Stubbs of Manchester Metropolitan University) showed that institutions are beginning to realise the potential of 'big data' for monitoring student progress – though it was acknowledged that such usage required a number of ethical issues to be worked through.

The examples of analyses in this chapter are illustrative of the potential (and limitations) of institutional data. They represent only a minute sample of what can be done and should be treated as illustrating the kinds of analysis that can be undertaken, without any pretence that they are exhaustive or even representative. The point of the chapter, above all, is to suggest a way of thinking about the kinds of data that may be available in a particular institution and how they might be exploited.

The work conducted during the *Second Year Experience Project* unearthed a number of sources of data that, in their different ways, throw light on the second-year experience:

- student record system (background and achievement data)
- institutional survey of students prior to their final year
- survey conducted by the Liverpool Students Union (LSU)
- attendance records in a faculty
- advice Centre data (anonymised) from the LSU
- anecdotal (and anonymised) evidence from Student Counselling and Well-being staff.

At the institutional level, the use with first- and second-year students of a survey mirroring the National Student Survey (NSS)[1] showed that across the case study institution, the second-year students had the lowest response rate, though in the majority of faculties the difference between the first and second years was slight. There is a hint in the figures of a possible diminution of students' engagement. A more marked difference was seen between first- and second-year students when they responded to the item 'Overall, I am satisfied with the quality of the course': the level of satisfaction was markedly lower for the second-year students across the university at 81.2 per cent compared with the first-year figure of 87.2 per cent.[2] As with the NSS, the mirror survey offers students the opportunity to add comments about their experience. Analysis of the comments using the Leximancer software showed that concepts such as 'university', 'year', 'coursework' and 'feedback' shifted from being seen as favourable to being seen as unfavourable, and the likelihood of concepts such as 'module' and 'timetable' being mentioned in a negative context became much higher (Zaitseva, Milsom and Stewart, 2013).

The Advice Centre at the LSU collects data on the issues that students raise with it. The number of inquiries during the academic year 2010–2011 was small relative to the total population of students, but data show that the level of advice-seeking was higher in the second year than it was in the first. There was a marked rise in the incidence of academic appeals, matters relating to personal mitigating circumstances and assessment outcomes, and complaints about the course. There was a small rise in issues relating to academic misconduct, and – not unexpectedly – a fall in the number of inquiries about changing course. Student recourse to the Advice Centre varied between faculties, which is the kind of signal that should alert a self-evaluating institution to the possibility of differences in the way that faculties (or perhaps sections of them) approach the student experience. It was noticeable from the data that academic programmes which had evidence of 'slumping' at some time were disproportionately represented in inquiries relating to academic matters, even though the numbers were again small.

One of the case study institution's faculties makes a particular point of monitoring student attendance. Data for the academic year 2009–2010 show that attendance level was lower for second-year students than for that in the other two years of the honours degree programme and in the pre-honours foundation year (Table 7.1).

Data may be less than ideal

Data collected for one purpose may not have a focus that is ideal for a different purpose. This can lead to challenges in respect of converting the data available into usable information. In the course of the *Second Year Experience Project*'s work, it was found that data categories were not always suitable for the analyses of an institutional researcher. The following three examples illustrate the point:

Table 7.1 Attendance data from one faculty for the academic year 2009–2010

Year	N of unique classes	N of expected attendances	N of actual attendances	Percentage attendance
Year 0 (Foundation)	48	6,144	4,223	68.7
Year 1	247	19,407	14,862	76.6
Year 2	164	7,247	4,813	66.4
Year 3	224	11,724	8,281	70.6

- Ethnicity was recorded in the student record system as White, Black and minority ethnic (BME) and as variants on 'unknown'. Since there is likely to be institutional interest in a more finely disaggregated analysis of outcomes related to ethnicity, such 'collapsing' of categories of ethnicity is less than optimal.
- The student record system overwrites a student's original mark where the student has undertaken the assessment again ('re-sat' it), almost always in an attempt to redeem an original failure.
- The coding of modules in use at the beginning of the *Second Year Experience Project* made it difficult to ascertain the level of the module in the student record system, since the modules were labelled in the form ABCDE1234, with 1 indicating the level of the module. When a student's record contained a mixture of levels within a year (e.g. when re-sat Level 4 modules were mixed in with Level 5 modules), separating out the Level 5 module performances was very time-consuming, since running a sort on the module codes would not achieve this. During the course of the project, the module codes had to be renumbered to take account of the re-designation of levels in the Framework for Higher Education Qualifications in England, Wales and Northern Ireland,[3] and the opportunity was taken to place the digit indicating the level of study first – for example, 4234ABCDE – which is much more helpful to the analyst.

Given the complexity of student record data and the need to produce findings sufficiently quickly to inform action, there is often a need to trade-off exactness against timeliness. For example, it would be useful to an institution if it could predict with reasonable accuracy whether students' marks would show a dip from first-year levels. Analysis of student records showed that, for a substantial minority of the larger programmes at the case study institution, there was a dip in mean marks between Years 1 and 2. Longitudinal and cross-sectional data were analysed in order to ascertain whether the latter (having the advantage of a more rapid production of results) would make an adequate proxy for the former: the analyses suggested that there was roughly a 70 per cent overlap between the two methods (Yorke and Zaitseva, 2013). If an analysis of this sort is used to inform practice, account has to be taken of the extent to which the programme allows students to exercise choice of modules. The 'homogeneity index' constructed as part of this study showed that the majority of the programmes considered were largely homogeneous as regards student enrolment on modules. However, a small minority of programmes allowed a fairly high level of choice of module, which would weaken the predictive power of the cross-sectional analysis.

'Big picture' analyses

The survey of students' experiences by the Higher Education Policy Institute and the Higher Education Academy in the UK (Soilemetzidis et al., 2014) has painted a large-scale picture which contains a number of 'messages' for policy-makers and institutional leaders. In the data available in support of the findings, a comparison of the experiences of first- and second-year students[4] suggests that, broadly, second-year students are marginally less well served than their first-year counterparts. The data made available do not allow a more penetrating analysis of the differences between first- and second-year students' experiences (e.g. at the level of, say, subject area or demographic characteristic), and the problem with heavily aggregated data is that any variation between sub-groups tends to be swamped. The challenge for the researcher is to choose a level of aggregation in a dataset that is optimal for the particular research question being asked.

Carefully selected groupings of data can reveal features of institutional provision that are often not noticeable at programme or module level because of small numbers. If data from the programme can be imagined in terms of the waves on an ocean, data at the level of the institution can be imagined as a great ocean current such as the Gulf Stream. An analysis of data from students who first enrolled in the academic year 2009–2010 illustrates the point.

Given the focus of this book is on the second-year experience of students, the analysis presented here concentrates on the relative performance of students in their first two years of full-time study. The criterion for inclusion in the analysis is that the students should have attempted at least 96 credits (out of the expected 120) in each year. Some students excluded from the analysis did not complete their first or second year of enrolled study (using the 96-credit criterion); some repeated part or all of their first-year studies; some transferred to other programmes; and some completed the single (first) year which was all that they had committed to undertake. The analysis covers seven programmes for which the original enrolment was in excess of 100 students, plus three composites of similar total enrolment in sciences, engineering and humanities, where the programmes could clearly be identified as lying within one of these broad categories. The analysis is based on the results from 1,203 students.

The question being asked of the dataset was the extent to which background variables (largely demographic) might be associated with a decline in mean mark between the first and second years of study. The data were analysed at programme or broad category level, then for the whole of the student sample.

Table 7.2 Analyses of 1,203 student records from seven programmes and three composites, mainly by demographic variables

Variable	Prog A	Prog B	Prog C	Prog D	Prog E	Prog F	Prog G	Science	Engineering	Humanities	All
	N = 104	N = 90	N = 95	N = 171	N = 141	N = 89	N = 129	N = 125	N = 165	N = 94	N = 1,203
Gender	NSD	NSD	NSD	NSD	NSD	NSD	NSD	NSD		NSD	Males more likely to slump than females ($p = .046$, Cramer's $V = .059$, $p = .040$)
Age (young/ mature)	NSD	NSD	NSD	NSD	Mature more likely than young to slump ($p = .024$)		NSD	NSD	NSD	NSD	Mature more likely than young to slump ($p = .016$, Cramer's $V = .072$, $p = .013$)

Ethnicity	NSD	NSD	NSD	White more likely than BME to slump ($p = .046$)	NSD	NSD	NSD	NSD between White and BME. Unknown ethnicity perform significantly worse ($p = .002$, Cramer's $V = .101$, $p = .002$)
Tariff points	Higher tariff points less likely to slump ($p = 021$)	NSD	Higher tariff points less likely to slump ($p = 008$)	NSD	NSD	NSD	NSD	Higher tariff points less likely to slump ($p = .047$; effect size $= .016$)
Disability							NSD	NSD

(continued)

Table 7.2 (continued)

	Prog A	Prog B	Prog C	Prog D	Prog E	Prog F	Prog G	Science	Engineering	Humanities	All
Entry qualifications	'Other' with 'Other HE & Professional' more likely to slump than A-Level ($p = .029$)	NSD		NSD	NSD (though graduate entry performs notably badly)	NSD	NSD	NSD	NSD		Higher qualified perform less well than A-Level & equiv. ($p = .002$, Cramer's $V = .112$, $p = .002$)
Domicile	NSD	NSD			NSD	NSD	NSD		NSD		Outside EU perform less well than UK and EU ($p = .000$, Cramer's $V = .112$, $p = .000$)

Notes

A blank cell indicates where numbers are too small in a contributing group to permit statistical analysis (e.g. too few females in Engineering). NSD = no significant difference; BME = Black and minority ethnic; EU = European Union; HE = higher education.

The results are presented in summary form in Table 7.2.[5] For some background variables, there were too few students to produce meaningful analyses at the level of the programme or broad category (e.g. too few females in the Engineering programmes that are combined in the composite), hence the blank cells in the table.

Table 7.2 shows that there is no strong association between background variables and 'slumping': where there is a difference worthy of consideration, the effect sizes are small. An analogous analysis using a different selection of student records produced a broadly similar result. In other words, the very modest associations make it necessary to look elsewhere for more compelling influences on slumping – which is a worthwhile finding in itself, since it helps to avoid undertaking relatively unprofitable investigations. It is possible, of course, that in other analyses and/or in other institutions there will be a stronger association between demographic variables and indexes of student achievement – for example, there is consistent evidence that BME students tend to gain lower classes of degree than their White counterparts (e.g. Broecke and Nicholls, 2007; Cousin *et al.*, 2008; Equality Challenge Unit, 2012) and that minority students in the US achieve less well than their White counterparts in the US (e.g. Carnevale and Strohl, 2013; Center for Community College Student Engagement [CCCSE], 2014).

'Looking elsewhere' led the *Second Year Experience Project* team towards looking at data (largely qualitative) such as student perceptions of their experiences, perceptions of both academic and support staff, and at issues relating to curriculum design and implementation. As was noted in Chapters 3, 4 and 6, a variety of influences could bear, differently for different students, on achievement; among them are the following:

- The dissipation of the excitement of the first year.
- Perception that the second year was less important (despite it counting 25 per cent to the honours degree classification) and – perhaps consequentially – as offering greater opportunity for social activities.
- Marks lower than expected, producing demoralisation.
- Curriculum design that concentrated, for different reasons, on the first and final years with the middle year lacking a clear character – a bit 'betwixt and between'.
- A step-change in difficulty (with various perceptions of the nature of the change, including leaving the shelter of repetition of A-Level study and the challenge of being faced with 'hard-grind' modules such as research methods as a forerunner of final-year project work).

The last of the above points prompted an analysis of seven programmes – four in which there was a persistent tendency of marks in the second year to dip below those of the first year, and three where there was not. The A-Level subjects taken by students entering the university in 2010 and 2011 were combined and tallied according to whether (a) they were a close match with the subject pursued at the university, (b) they might have relevance to the programme of study and (c) where there seemed little or no relevance. The categorisation was cross-checked and a few minor disagreements resolved. Table 7.3 shows that, on the evidence from these seven programmes, there seems to be no association between the A-Level subjects studied and a decline in marks in the second year. A qualitative investigation could be undertaken to test this tentative inference.

The point of this investigation is to demonstrate that the data in institutional records can be mined in order to test hypotheses about student achievement and other matters. The data for this particular investigation were not particularly finely delineated, but were 'good enough' to suggest that a 'folk-wisdom' hypothesis connecting performance decrement to prior study at A-Level might not be supported and that research inquiries might with profit be directed elsewhere. However, as measures of performance, marks do not have the reliability that is popularly and implicitly ascribed to them (see Yorke, 2008), and ideally the net needs to be cast more widely for indicators of performance.

Taken in the round and acknowledging that the data unearthed within the university are of variable quality (as is likely to be the case in many institutions), the 'big picture' of students' second-year experience can be summarised as follows:

- Background demographic data appear to have little influence on the propensity of students' performances to dip in the second year: where statistics do suggest a connection, the effect is small.
- A number of indicators point to the possibility of a diminution of engagement in the second year, which is reversed in subsequent years.
- Explanations for weakness in second-year engagement and/or performance are more likely to be found in students' experiences on their programmes than in demographics, which is why attention needs to be paid to qualitative and quantitative data relating to the student experience.

Table 7.3 The relationship, for seven programmes, between first- and second-year performances and previously studied A-Levels

Programme category	N of students	N of A-Levels	Year 2 lower?	Fit with A-Level?		
				(%) Yes	Possibly (%)	No (%)
Humanities/ Social Science 1	95	296	Yes	0.0	59.2	40.8
Science 1	52	158	Yes	24.5	39.6	35.8
Social Science 1	286	907	Yes	28.3	31.1	40.6
Social Science 2	181	552	Yes	32.4	20.5	47.2
Arts 1	90	274	No	32.1	34.6	33.2
Science 2	36	93	No	32.3	22.6	45.2
Arts 2	47	138	No	39.7	12.8	47.5

'Employability' has featured strongly in higher education policy in the UK and elsewhere, as governments seek to capitalise economically on their higher education systems (for varied perspectives on the issue see, among many possible examples, Department for Education and Skills, 2003 [UK]; Twenty-first Century Workforce Commission, 2000 [US]; Australian Education Council: Mayer Committee, 1992 [Australia]). Many institutions in the UK express this in their own policies, as is evident from their websites. Institutional data can be mined to identify the extent to which policy of this kind can be captured in practice across the institution. A small-scale study of six programmes in the case study institution which were not overtly 'vocational' examined the assessment methods in use, using the documentation available from the university's module catalogue to identify issues that were subsequently explored with the respective programme leaders. Analysis showed that programmes varied in the extent to which 'soft skills' (as opposed to academic achievement) were embodied and that, in general, more was being done to foster employability than might casually be assumed (see Tyrer *et al.*, 2013). The exploitation of data of this kind, with sampling undertaken more comprehensively, can enable an assessment to be made of the extent to which an institution's espoused policy is converted into practice.

The data warehouse: a case study from the UvA

The background

The UvA has its origins in the Athenaeum Illustre (1632) and, with more than 30,000 students and 5,000 employees, and an annual budget of €600 million, is one of the largest general research universities in Europe (see Box 7.1). Despite this, it faces real pressure. Government's cost-cutting measures combined with new responsibilities in the form of performance agreements and increasing student numbers mean that universities are facing a permanent challenge to raise their profile. Dutch universities also need to become more competitive and more entrepreneurial, which means being better informed. Investments and policy decisions, executive council meetings and quality policy all call for information that is fast, consistent, reliable and integrated. Despite all the data recorded by institutions in a country with such a highly developed administrative culture as the Netherlands, effective *information* has still been lacking far too often. Data have typically been recorded for operational processes such as the payment of salaries, the awarding of degree certificates, the purchase of equipment, but rarely for the benefit of governance or management. Since the late 1980s, when Dutch universities were given greater independence but also more responsibilities, the UvA has been working to improve its management information.

Institutional research

In 1990, the UvA launched a Management Information project. The project group brought together policy staff and data analysts from various domains.

Box 7.1   A sketch of the University of Amsterdam

Study programmes (open for intake as of September 2013)

- 57 Bachelor's programmes (3 taught in English), including 1 joint degree with the VU University Amsterdam
- 92 Master's programmes (66 taught in English), including 20 Research Master's programmes (17 taught in English) and 8 Dual Master's programmes (2 taught in English)
- 23 Teacher training programmes (exclusively taught in Dutch)
- 10 Executive Master's programmes (3 taught in English), including 1 joint degree with Universitet Aarhus Denemarken

Students (reference date: 1 October 2013)

- Total enrolled: 31,123
- Number of first-year students: 8,316*

*Number of students enrolling at the UvA for the first time (at the Bachelor's, pre-Master's or Master's level)

Research in 2013

- Number of PhDs awarded: 517
- Number of scientific publications: 9,792

UvA employees in 2013, excluding the Amsterdam Medical Center (AMC):

- 2,321 academic members of staff (1,801 full-time equivalent [FTE]), excluding doctoral candidates
- 2,375 members of staff in non-academic positions (1,869 FTE)

They were tasked with creating integrated management information based on the administrative and other sources to which they had access. They were also authorised to collect and analyse new information where necessary. The work that had to be done was new to these officers, and some of them went to the US to get familiar with a profession and institutional research that was already well established in the American higher education institutions, but still less known in Europe at that time (see, e.g. Saupe, 1990; Terenzini, 1993). Institutional research is 'research conducted within an institution of higher education in order to provide information which supports planning, policy formation and decision making' (Saupe, 1990, p. 1).

Similar developments were underway at other Dutch universities during the 1990s, and therefore specialists in institutional research (and even whole departments) began to emerge among university policy staff. These people sought contact with each other in order to share information and best practice (Hoekstra and Vendel, 1999). In 2001, they joined forces and founded the Dutch Association for Institutional Research (DAIR) (Hoekstra, 2005). Increasing competition in some areas played a role in triggering greater cooperation and coordination in other parts of the universities. This became evident in the joint development and application of definitions and even wide-ranging databases of key indicators, especially in the areas of education, research and staff.

Since its development, institutional research has made great progress, including at the UvA, in the analysis of data for policy use and in enhancing understanding of, and access to, administrative databases. Data on student progress became more reliable, surveys were conducted and analysed more systematically and where possible linked to administrative data, and trends were identified earlier and more effectively. But the information was often still based on manual work and on collating data from various sources and administrative records. Although much of this was 'good' data, it was also often what is described as 'bad' or 'ugly' and needed to be cleaned up before being processed and analysed. The work was time-consuming and vulnerable to error. In addition, new policy issues would often call for the creation of new databases. There were also still various different data domains, which were accessed using different definitions at different times. Discussions were frequently dominated by issues relating to the reliability of the data rather than the actual trends the data revealed.

Data warehouse

Over time, the solution to this continual need to struggle with data was increasingly sought in technological enhancements and most importantly in the emerging concept of the data warehouse (Rome, 2004). According to an oft-quoted definition by Ralph Kimball, a data warehouse is 'a copy of transaction data specially structured for query and analysis' (Kimball, 1996, p. 310). Since then, other definitions have been devised, each time providing a better approximation of the fact that a data warehouse is about two things. The first of these is *institutional data*: the data warehouse contains data from an institution's own records as well as data about the institution from national sources. Second, a data warehouse is slightly different from a conventional database in that data are stored and *categorised for the purpose of reporting and analysis*. The primary function of a data warehouse is to integrate all institutional data and ensure consistency within it.

This may seem straightforward and even obvious, but in practice it proves difficult. This is because the data usually originates from different records and systems, which makes it a technical challenge to integrate this data correctly within a system that also needs to perform well and quickly. However, it is equally challenging to attempt to bring all of the different owners of definitions, systems and processes, each involved in different ways, into line with each other. Finally, of course, it is also a challenge to identify the lowest common denominator in terms of the need for information and the expectations of executive officers and managers at different organisational levels.

The UvA took on these challenges and succeeded in building a data warehouse, whose development principles are given in Box 7.2. In 2009, the first release of UvAdata was completed and, following a positive evaluation by an external party, approved by the university. Since that time, UvAdata has issued several new releases and now includes almost 100 reports with countless options to expand or drill down.

UvAdata: management information online

UvAdata, the data warehouse for UvA's executive officers, managers and their support staff, has now been running for several years and is acknowledged within the university as a legitimate source of management information. But what is it exactly?

In technical terms, UvAdata is a data warehouse built in SAP BW.[6] It provides access to the most important UvA-wide records, as well as to national databases and university survey records. UvAdata contains the reports presented via the SAP Enterprise Portal. Finally, extensive user documentation is also part of UvAdata. This takes the form of a wiki that can be called up from every report.

Box 7.2   The seven development principles of UvAdata

1   Transparent: All authorised users have access to general, reliable and clear information.

2   Confidential: At detailed and transaction levels, users have access to data only within their own area of jurisdiction.

3   General: Centrally managed reports are distributed via the portal. These reports are self-explanatory, the definitions and calculation rules they use are integrated within them, and they are in principle of interest to the entire institutional community.

4   Analytical: Focused on analyses and strategic information, where possible transcending individual domains and where necessary capable of being divided into detailed information for analysis.

5   Reproducible: Targeting reproducible data, accessed based on discrete periods and frozen archives.

6   Perspective: Focused on discontinuous, gradual changes and extensions (releases).

7   Performance: Performance – in other words, the speed at which the reports work – is always an evaluation criterion for users and therefore also for UvAdata.

For authorised users, UvAdata is a reporting tool that can be easily accessed from within the portal environment, without the need for any special software. Because UvAdata has so much data at the lowest level of aggregation, the UvA enforces an extremely strict authorisation policy. Everyone who has access to UvAdata, which includes almost 500 executive officers, managers, controllers and policy staff, can access the same extensive but generalised data for the whole university. Based on the need-to-know principle, managers and others have access only to the often very private detailed information within their own area of jurisdiction.

The information is categorised according to five information domains: education, research, finances, personnel and accommodation. There is also a domain with summary management reports. Users have the option of exporting data to Microsoft Excel, for example.

All of the reports have a unified presentation. They work according to the same principles.

1   They open with a *Monitor*: an overview/graphic and a table containing the subject information. This can be the development of the enrolment over the last five years, the staff costs, the number of PhD students, and so on.
2   A click leads through to a flexible report that, like a pivot table, gives the user all kinds of possibilities to analyse. All numbers can be broken down by characteristics like age, sex, organisational units, and so on.
3   A further click leads to a flexible report where the *authorised* user can drill down to the lowest level of detail, the *atomic* data. These might be the names of the staff members or students, the exact financial figures, and so on.

Information domains

The domains contained in UvAdata are represented diagrammatically in a 'Management Information Rail Map' (Figure 7.1). This is an artist's impression of the available management information in the university. The 'stations' are the subjects of the reports.

The *Education* domain contains the background data on all students, monthly updated data on their study progress, their tuition fee payments, the results of national student surveys as well as intake and study success data for students from the other Dutch universities (benchmarks).

In the Personnel and Finances domains, UvAdata has a lot of data on the research effort. The results of this effort can be found in the *Research* domain: the publications are sorted by type (academic, popular, etc.), by title, author's name and research projects. Data about PhD students include their success rates and the professors involved.

The data about *Personnel* relate to staff composition and development, staff turnover, salary, absences due to sickness, leave and time-sheets. One important perspective is a linking of personnel to finances (e.g. average personnel costs in relation to duties). National benchmark data are also included in this domain.

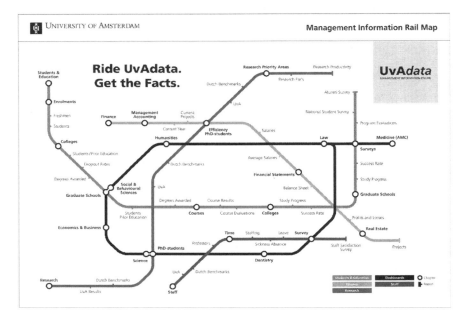

Figure 7.1 University of Amsterdam: Management information rail map

The most important data in the *Finances* domain relate to the internal financial management of the university and the different faculties and units. Budgets, implementation, forecasts and internal resource allocation are all displayed according to the UvA's EU-certified costing model.

In addition to the data from these domains referred to above, there are also reports that provide support for issues relating to *Accommodation* (categorised by building, floor area according to different definitions, purpose of use) and on the status of investments in the long-term accommodation plan.

The Executive Board and the deans draw upon the above data and information in their six-monthly Periodic Executive Council (Periodiek Bestuurlijk Overleg [PBO]) meetings. This domain is known as the management reports (*Dashboards*) and is separate within UvAdata. Developments raised on the agenda in the PBOs can now also be monitored in the months leading up to such meetings.

Study success: an example of the use of UvAdata

The UvA has been pursuing an active study success policy for some years now. The main focus is on improving study success rates during the Bachelor's phase. Concrete objectives and target figures for 2014 are defined in a Performance Agreement between the university and the Dutch Ministry of Education. According to this agreement, at least 70 per cent of students from the 2010 cohort re-registering for the degree programme after the first academic year must have obtained their Bachelor's degree within four years.

For the UvA study success is an important key performance indicator (KPI), and therefore it has been built in UvAdata as a *Dashboard*. Figure 7.2 shows that the study success of the UvA cohort 2004 after four years was 48.1 per cent and that the figures increased to 66.2 per cent for the 2009 cohort (the latest for which four-year data are available). This is almost the level that was agreed upon for the 2010 cohort.

The Dashboard has been used in three ways:

1   The well-defined data have been discussed in Executive Council meetings and in faculties. It prevented debates about the definition of the data, and so on (single version of the truth).
2   The Dashboard has been used to analyse situations. Groups that had succeeded or dropped out could be analysed because all numbers can be broken down by sex, age, type of prior education, nationality and more. The performance of these groups has been compared with that of other groups (from the UvA or other Dutch universities). UvAdata gives access to the national benchmark database as well.

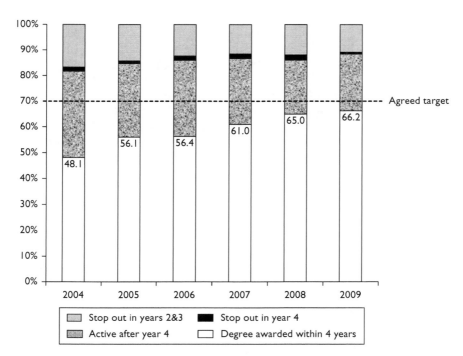

Figure 7.2 The Dashboard showing study success for UvA cohorts commencing between 2004 and 2009

3   Authorised users have used the possibility to drill down from the Dashboard to the *atomic data,* the names and numbers of the students that were involved – this helped them to understand the Dashboards and the definition and made educational interventions easier.

The benefits of UvAdata

The UvA now has at its disposal a data warehouse that is gradually being rolled out. Of course, its construction, development and management cost money. However, for the UvA, these costs are significantly outweighed by the benefits. These are threefold: management decisions are better informed and the management culture is therefore becoming more business-like, support services are professionalised and there is quality enhancement in administrative record-keeping.

UvAdata's primary role is to provide empirical information to the Board and management. What matters, therefore, is not only the number of times that UvAdata is consulted (which is itself monitored) but also more importantly the number of decisions and justifications of policy in which UvAdata plays a role. UvAdata is resulting in the development of a shared language within the UvA. A key benefit is, therefore, the extent to which discussions within the executive committees can be accelerated and made more professional because of the ability to use a single language and access clear-cut statistics.

The managers who were early adopters of technological advances have quickly become conversant with UvAdata. Because these people had an urgent need for data, UvAdata served an important and immediate purpose for them. These early users have also been the people who have led the way and encouraged colleagues to use it.

Many reports that were previously compiled by central units or by staff within the faculties and units (or indeed by both) can now be obtained simply from UvAdata as standard reports. This saves time for controllers, programme coordinators, policy staff, administrators and others whose job it is to collect data for management purposes.

Findings from UvAdata frequently lead to useful reassessments of the way in which information is managed at the UvA. If it proves extremely difficult to construct specific data, enhancements are made to the corporate administration and the administrative organisation, where possible. Another additional benefit of UvAdata is the cleansing effect it has on university records. Now, data are viewed and assessed by many more people and in much clearer contexts, and both the people who take executive responsibility for the quality of the records and their support staff are more likely to ask questions and to do so in a more focused way. This means that errors are less likely to occur and, when they do occur, are corrected more rapidly, making the UvAdata more reliable.

Maximising the use of institutional data

Building a data warehouse involves coordinating definitions, improving administrative routines and cleaning up databases. When all of that has been done, researchers, policy staff and managers can then pose their own questions and conduct their own analyses, which will lead to an increase in the intellectual use of valuable administrative data (Yorke, 2006).

However, there will not be many people who have both the necessary skills and time to conduct institutional research. This kind of research remains necessary, if only to evaluate, for instance, policy interventions in education, or develop policy theories on such issues as the relationship between students' previous education and their study success, and so on. These policy theories are ultimately what justify the need for meaningful monitors that are more than simply counting machines.

It is anticipated that the development of reliable data warehouses will also lead to a reorientation for institutional research. Not only do users have access to increasing amounts of ever-more reliable information, but the data can also be applied in different ways, the most important of which is for forecasting. Trends that can be described can also be extrapolated, making policy scenarios more realistic. At its best, the work of institutional research influences changes in policy.

Perhaps more importantly, a shift may also occur in the target group. Until now, institutional research was targeted at executive officers and managers. However, the data on students now available in the data warehouse (e.g. background information, enrolment and study progress data, and survey results) open up the possibility for direct and indirect communication between the data warehouse and students. Institutional research already has profile information on students, which means the likelihood of their completing their studies successfully and on time is known. The combination of this likelihood and actual study progress, which is monitored in the data warehouse, provides information that can be of major importance for students. The earlier that problems or patterns can be identified that may result in drop-out or delays, the greater the chance that the students involved will be able to do something about it. A data warehouse like UvAdata can be used as a source to do this kind of 'big data' analysis.

In the longer term, UvAdata will be used more intensively – partly because it is now there to be used, but also because the UvA is strongly promoting its use. Indeed, UvA is working to improve the planning and control cycle and enhance control at all levels. The new Strategic Plan will feature key progress indicators more prominently than before, and UvAdata will need to incorporate these more effectively in its reports to all departments and levels. Management information will become an unavoidable part of the work of managers and executive officers and of the institutional discourse, ultimately in order to become information used by the entire academic community – as Henry Louis Gates (Jr) put it, in an IBM/ Linux commercial, 'Collecting data is the first step toward wisdom, but sharing data is the first step toward community'.

Getting the message across

There is a risk in using institutional data (or data from other sources, for that matter) that the analytical output may be presented in a form that the recipients find difficult to understand. A compelling example was presented in 2010 at the Institutional Research conference held at Dublin City University. Peter Gray, on secondment from the US Naval Academy to Oxford Brookes University, showed an example of regression analyses of marks from modules based on nine years of data, whose purpose was to inform senior managers. Anyone lacking a fairly sophisticated command of statistical methodology would have found the analyses to be impenetrable. The medium was getting in the way of the message. Gray presented a much simpler analysis which was far more intelligible to the intended audience and which was 'good enough' to inform possible action.[7] A number of institutions contributing to the 'What Works?' programme[8] have taken advantage of the development of analytical software to produce reports on aspects of institutional functioning that are readily intelligible to their audiences, e.g. York St John University has produced a scattergram showing how its performance on both widening participation and retention compares with the performances of other institutions (see Matthews, 2014).

Ewell and Jones (1994, p. 16) warned of the danger of over-complicating data collection and the production of indicators:

> Many promising indicator systems fail simply because they are too expensive, too complex, too time-consuming, or too politically costly to implement. Often the simplest is the best, even if it seems less technically attractive.

The characteristics of data and analytical output being 'good enough' (Simon [1957] used the term 'satisficing' in this respect) need to be unpacked. The data may be less than ideal when used for a purpose not originally envisaged – for example, using overwritten student mark data when original marks would be preferable because the work required to disinter the original mark data would not be worth the effort involved.[9] They may, nevertheless, be good enough for the purpose at hand. Being 'good enough' implies that the odds attached to the likelihood that the analysis is not due to chance may fall some way short of the $p < .05$ level of statistical significance (assuming that the conditions for statistical testing can be met): the practicalities of institutional functioning may be satisfied by relatively slender odds – indeed, anything better than an even chance may suffice for practical action (Yorke, 1995).

It is possible to offer in this chapter merely a few indicative examples of the way in which institutional data can be drawn upon in the service of policy and practice. What can be done with such data is limited only by the imagination.

Key points

- Institutions probably possess more data than is generally appreciated. The challenge is to find a way of making best use of what is available.
- A 'data warehouse' offers opportunities for maximising the use of data, but takes time to establish.

- In analysing statistical data relating to student experience and achievement, it is important to select a level of aggregation that is appropriate to the research question being asked.
- Data collected for one purpose may not be perfect for other purposes: nevertheless, they may be 'good enough' for operational use.

Notes

1 The National Student Survey (NSS) in the UK solicits responses from students in the final year of their programme and is administered externally on behalf of the higher education sector.
2 In three schools there was a very small increase in the satisfaction level, which together were swamped by larger declines elsewhere.
3 At the beginning of the Project, Level 1 related to the first year of study on a bachelor's degree. Subsequently, the Framework for Higher Education Qualifications in England, Wales and Northern Ireland redesignated this as Level 4. The Frameworks for Higher Education Qualifications in England, Wales and Northern Ireland (2008) can be accessed via http://www.qaa.ac.uk/publications. The Framework for Qualifications of Higher Education Institutions in Scotland (revised 2014) can be accessed via http://www.qaa.ac.uk/publications/information-and-guidance.
4 The data are available as an Excel spreadsheet at http://www.hepi.ac.uk/2014/05/21/hepi-hea-2014-student-academic-experience-survey/.
5 Since Table 7.2 is a summary, a number of qualifications have to be ignored in the presentation of the results. The sampling throughout does not meet the requirements for parametric statistical analysis, and so the significance levels (where given) for tariff points have to be treated as indicative only. The other variables have been analysed by contingency tables, using the nonparametric chi-square test with the correction for continuity where appropriate. Analyses involving more than two groups (such as the various categories of entry qualification) occasionally suggested that a sharper picture of where differences lie would be obtained by omitting categories where the number of cases was too low for valid contingency table analysis: this was done where appropriate. Regarding specific variables, disability was collapsed into two categories (no disability recorded and disability recorded, since numbers were too small to allow meaningful analyses with respect to types of disability); and domicile was treated as a binary variable (UK and Not UK) in the programme and composite analyses, but as a ternary variable (UK, EU outside UK and outside EU) for the analysis of the combined 1,203 cases.
6 Headquartered in Walldorf, Germany, with locations in many countries, SAP AG is one of the large companies in enterprise software and software-related services. The UvA uses SAP software for almost all of the university administrations. The SAP data warehouse was originally named SAP BIW (Business Information Warehouse), then abbreviated to SAP BW. SAP BW is developed by SAP to serve as a database that can be used for decision support.
7 Unfortunately, the PowerPoint presentation is no longer available.
8 The 'What Works? Student Retention and Success Change Programme' involves 13 varied universities in implementing initiatives over a three-year period which are designed to increase student retention and success. The programme is supported by the Paul Hamlyn Foundation and the Higher Education Academy (see http://www.heacademy.ac.uk/resources/detail/retention/PHF/retention_and_success_change_programme_2012–2015).
9 If the issue is sufficiently compelling, the institution might decide to change the way in which data are recorded.

Chapter 8

Listening for signals in the noise and acting on them

Mantz Yorke, Clare Milsom, Martyn Stewart and Elena Zaitseva

The complexity of the picture

The preceding chapters are testimony to the complexity inherent in the transition from first-year to second-year study and in the development of students' learning in the second year. Trying to make sense of it all is – in its own way – as challenging as extracting meaning from the 'blooming, buzzing confusion' that William James (1890: 488) envisaged a baby experiencing; working out what Samuel Beckett really meant to convey to a theatre audience when writing the multifaceted *Waiting for Godot*; or trying to detect the trace of a Higgs Boson among the thicket of curves and twirls recorded by the Large Hadron Collider. What this book has done is to point to a number of aspects of students' experience which can – in varying degrees – influence their success. Teachers, programmes, support services and institutions as a whole play a part, and it is probably uncommon for any single influence to determine whether an individual fulfils, or fails to fulfil, their potential.

It is abundantly evident that student achievement in the second year of full-time study is subject to a wide variety of influences. The influences may be personal or institutional and may extend to matters affecting the higher education system as a whole. In researching student experience and achievement, what one focuses on and the lens that is used together determine what one sees. The (severe) challenge for anyone researching student achievement in an institution is to find a way of integrating findings at different levels: for anyone seeking understanding across institutions, there is the additional challenge of accommodating differing cultures and structures. In the technical sense of the term, the education of students is chaotic: initiatives in support of students' success have to be construed in probabilistic terms, with some activities 'working' better to achieve success than others – and for reasons that are not always apparent.

The plethora of variables precludes the proffering of recommendations regarding practices that will guarantee greater success for second-year (or middle-year) students. The focus of this chapter is on issues that merit consideration at different levels within higher education and that are connected in one way or another with student success. The 'flow' is broad from 'the student experience' to the higher education system as a whole, though there are cross-currents and eddies because influences interact.

A shocking experience?

Some students experience shock when the reality of the second-year curriculum becomes apparent. The sense of shock may stem from having had an 'easy ride' in the first year:

- They may have in part been revisiting academic content studied in school or college.
- They may have carried over study methods that they had found adequate for success prior to higher education, without realising that higher education would demand of them something different.
- The curriculum may not have sent strong enough signals that students should exercise autonomy from the start of their programme (though some students clearly expect to undertake independent study, which is not the same thing).
- They may have inferred that all they needed to do was to pass the year in order to progress, without appreciating that passing was a necessary but not sufficient condition for success in the following years (which, under current UK programme structures, are the years that determine the class of the honours degree).

Suggestions for the resolution of issues such as these can be found in Chapters 2, 5 and 6.

Issue	Who might act
Encouraging student autonomy in learning in Year 1	Curriculum designers supported by quality assurance
Preparing students for the second-year demands	Programme leaders, teachers
Providing early formative and helpful feedback in order to help students appreciate expected standards	Teachers
Anticipating students' shock at receiving lower marks/grades than expected	Teachers

The long summer break

In the UK, the summer break at the end of the first year of higher education has become lengthy. With Easter being late in 2014, some institutions concluded their formal teaching sessions in early April, with the summer term being used for revision and assessment. Students do not return to their institutions until late September or early October: the break has plenty of potential for them to forget what they have learned. While acknowledgement must be made of students' use of this time for replenishing their bank balances or for widening their horizons through travel, institutions may want to find ways of retaining students' engagement with their studies.

At minimum, contact could be maintained via newsletter or website: in addition to formal information about requirements (which might otherwise get forgotten), such communication could contain advice and guidance relating to second-year studies (see, for example, the website on sophomore initiatives that has been produced by Minnesota State University Mankato[1]). Some of the advice could derive from students further on in the same programme.

More boldly, the opportunity might be taken to engage students in some form of relevant academic activity (e.g. a project, a group inquiry, preparation for a study module) which would mean that they did not commence their second year from a standing start. Relevant material can be found in Chapter 5.

Issue	Who might act
Bridging the summer break	Year 2 module leaders, Year 2 tutors. Institutional policy-makers

Induction to the second year

Even if institutions seek to mitigate the problems associated with the summer break (such as the 'shock to the system') by methods such as those of the preceding section, an induction to the second year has potential advantages. Indeed, Maguire (2006) applied a critical phase analysis to degree programmes in Environmental Sciences at the University of Ulster and in a brief article identified the importance of induction at the start of *each year* of the programmes as preparation for the changing requirements and standards of the respective years. She also pointed to the need to cater for students who enter the programmes' second year directly – to which can be added those students who resume studies after a substantial break. Wilson (2013) describes an induction day for students moving from Level 4 of a foundation degree[2] which had been taught in a further education college to Level 5 in Edge Hill University.

In Chapter 1, evidence was presented illustrating that students on some programmes attained lower marks in their second year than they did in the first. In part, this could be due to a misplaced belief that they were doing well (because their first-year marks were good), only to be set back by the realities of the second-year curriculum – which might demand a heavier and more intense workload than students expect. There is scope here for running a session reviewing learning from the first year and relating it to second-year expectations. Chapters 5 and 6, particularly, deal with clarifying academic demand from differing perspectives.

Issue	Who might act
Making the demands of Year 2 explicit	Academic department, programme team, Year 2 tutors, student support services

Standards

Qualifications frameworks are not explicit about standards; nor are the subject benchmarks published by the Quality Assurance Agency for Higher Education in the UK. While this is not a matter for surprise, given the need to cater for programme variation between and within subject disciplines, standards are primarily referenced against the norms that have become established in disciplinary areas (sometimes in conjunction with professional, statutory and regulatory bodies). If, as seems quite often to be the case, the standards expected of students in their second year constitute a step up from those in the first year, how can these be conveyed?

It is well known that statements of expected learning outcomes and assessment criteria are difficult to interpret on their own. Anonymised exemplars of student work of different standards can help to explain what is expected and may be more powerful if the students work through them in groups in order to identify strengths and weaknesses. Working in this way comes close to the use of 'crits' in Art & Design. An alternative is to get students to assess their peers' work formatively: Gibbs (1999) provides an interesting example from Engineering where such formative 'marking' engendered a notable improvement in summative assessments. The purpose of activities such as these is to improve the signalling of standards so that students appreciate as clearly as possible what is expected of them: Sadler, since his widely cited article (Sadler, 1987), has been assiduous in asserting the importance of students internalising standards in order to develop their autonomy and capacity for self-regulation.

Chapter 2 deals with issues relating to qualifications frameworks, standards and curriculum design.

Issue	Who might act
Clarification of expected standards	Teaching staff, primarily; quality support staff

Student perspectives on learning

A key issue is the perspective that students bring to their studies. If students approach study with learning goals uppermost, then this ought to be manifested in their performance. If performance goals are uppermost, then good learning may or may not be associated – high achievers are more likely to benefit in this way. The danger here is that an emphasis on learning outcomes in curriculum specifications will lead students to aim for the specified outcomes at the expense of wider learning. While the narrow focus might make it easier for a student to gain high marks (i.e. achieving performance goals), it may militate against the broader learning that higher education curricula typically seek.

Students often exhibit behaviours that fit the circumstances of the time: for subject matter that attracts their commitment, they engage in 'deep' learning, whereas for material that they have to learn for some auxiliary purpose, 'surface' learning may be considered sufficient. Such behaviour is labelled 'strategic', but 'tactical' might be more appropriate as a term.

Miller and Parlett (1974) showed that some students were very aware of the signals sent out by their teachers (they were 'cue-conscious') and acted accordingly, whereas others were 'cue-deaf'. If students pick up signals that tell them that a key indicator of achievement is an upper second-class honours degree in the UK (or a grade-point average [GPA] of 3.00 in the US), then 'getting the grade' looms large as a personal objective. The balance tips towards performance goals and away from learning goals. A similar position obtains in respect of student learning in schools.

At a more local level, if students hear comments such as

- first year doesn't matter – you only need 40%,
- second year counts now – so make sure to attend, and
- that's important – it's worth 60% of module,

the implications for their behaviour are fairly obvious. How teachers approach their task signals – sometimes very powerfully – to students about how they, in turn, should approach their work.

A number of institutions in the UK are piloting trials of a GPA system that bears a number of similarities with practice in the US, but is not isomorphic. The institutions in the pilot vary in the way that they are considering its implementation: some, for instance, want to exclude first-year work from the calculation (on the grounds, broadly, that the first year is primarily about coming to terms with the demand of higher education, and weak performance should not adversely affect a student's overall outcome), whereas others see the inclusion of first-year work as part of the student's performance profile (and perhaps as a spur not to coast during that year). How students respond to the introduction of GPA will be worth researching.

Chapter 4 drew attention to changes in students' approaches to learning after the first year that may be disadvantageous in the longer term, particularly the slippage from mastery to performance goals. Given the pressures on students and the 'messages' they hear about achievement, this is not particularly surprising. There is probably a need for more research, both quantitative and qualitative and across the spectrum of subject disciplines, about the impact of teaching that emphasises the significance of learning goals and the importance of self-efficacy and metacognition in developing personal autonomy and self-regulation. At the level of the teaching team, it is worth identifying the extent to which students are enabled to push beyond their boundaries without losing their sense of security: one student quoted in Chapter 3 remarked on feeling secure but also pushed to extend the boundaries of their learning.

Evidence from Liverpool John Moores University showed that, in their second year, students tended to become more concerned with the applied side of the experience and development of practical skills, and that these were associated with higher levels of programme satisfaction. This probably reflects some internalisation of the 'employability' signal: potential employers are wont to inquire what applicants can offer in addition to their academic achievements. The fact that second-year marks contribute to the honours degree classification (albeit weighted at one-third of the final year's marks) is another relevant consideration.

An orientation to performance goals can be pernicious, in that students may feel that it is sufficient to achieve the curriculum's stated learning outcomes well: opportunities to locate their learning in a wider matrix can be missed by a narrowness of perspective. Narrowness may also be an issue where students complain about gaps in their formal timetable and do not see these as opportunities for working in the library or learning resource centre, or for engaging collaboratively with their fellow students.

A variety of angles relating to the encouragement of student learning are addressed in Chapters 3, 4, 5 and 6.

Issue	Who might act
Fostering of learning goals	All staff who are in contact
Being careful about the cues that students might pick up	with students

Institutional support

Students can be supported in many ways, both through formal institutional arrangements (such as study support systems and counselling services) and informally through academic and other staff, and friends and family. Some students – perhaps those who most need it – are not proactive in seeking help. Seeking help can be difficult, in that it is perceived to be an unacceptable admission of weakness: this may be a consequence of a cultural divide that is difficult to bridge directly – though with imagination there may be a way of working round the difficulty. When the research was being undertaken in the case study university, it was found that, despite experiencing some serious problems and being in need of professional pastoral support, some second-year students chose not to seek the support of tutors or of student counselling and well-being (perhaps based on misconceptions about the nature of these services), but to seek support from elsewhere. It might be that some greater structuring of such support would improve the situation – and perhaps provide a mechanism through which help could be provided without incurring a stigma.

Thomas (2012) sees the 'academic sphere' as the primary locus for a variety of interventions designed to enhance student retention and success. Academics in tutorial roles are well placed to offer advice regarding the choice of modules, given students' interests and post-university intentions. Some students in the empirical study commented on the relative shortage of tutorials in their second year which – if students are finding the going to be tough in their second year – hints at a possible need to re-balance the allocation of academic resources.

Those who teach student cohorts (and/or who act as personal tutors, especially if over a longer period than an academic year) are well placed to spot when students show signs of difficulty: if absences are being recorded, these can be early signals, as can requests for extensions to assignment deadlines and claims for dispensation regarding assessments because of illness or other kinds of misfortune (the term 'personal mitigating circumstances' is widely used in the UK). The difficulty, addressed later in this chapter, is that any individual member of staff may not know that other colleagues are having to deal with the same students' problems, and so the seriousness of the students' situations is not picked up quickly enough for appropriate support to be mobilised.

There may, however, be no obvious sign of students' distress even though they may not be performing to the best of their ability. Poor academic performance (e.g. if a student's marks in their second year are lower than those for their first) can lead to a vicious circle of stress and poor performance, yet the student may do enough to progress through the course without realising their full potential. In some cases, reference back to entry qualifications may provide a hint that such a cycle may be established – but this requires a data system readily capable of being interrogated by the concerned staff member.

Issues relating to student support are addressed primarily in Chapter 6.

Issue	Who might act
Students' need for support	All staff who are in contact with students

Students supporting students

Students who are further on in their programmes can have a lot to offer those who are following them through the programmes. The passing-on of 'lessons learned' can help students to avoid pitfalls their predecessors may have experienced. Peer mentoring requires training for the role – for example, to clarify the boundaries of what mentoring should cover. It has potential benefit for the mentors, too, in that the supporting of others has value when it comes to the submission of a curriculum vitae to a potential employer.

Self-help groups, such as those noted in Chapter 6, can be tremendously supportive. As with group projects, much learning can take place as students exchange ideas and contributions – though there are expectations, typically informal in self-help groups, that 'freeloading' is not acceptable. Again as with group projects, the implications for assessment may need to be worked through: if assignments are submitted on the basis of informal collaborative work, what view should the institution take?

Students can support students through a variety of social media, through students' unions, and by contributing to guidebooks on the student experience. From such a guidebook, Miller (2014) presents an extract that offers students in the US advice on avoiding the sophomore slump. Advice of this sort could be a very useful addition to the resources provided by the National Union of Students in the UK.

There is a range of issues relating to student support of fellow students: Chapter 6 is where coverage of these is mainly to be found.

Issue	Who might act
Friendship formation and 'belongingness'	Teachers, students
Collaborative work on assignments	Institution (via policy on collaboration and assessment)
Peer mentoring implementation	Programme leaders, Year 2 module leaders, Year 2 tutors
Peer mentoring training	Students Union, academic organisational unit
General advice regarding second-year study	National Union of Students in the UK, and similar organisations

More broadly, Tinto (1993), among others, has argued the importance of social integration. Thomas (2012), drawing on evidence from seven projects in the UK, has pointed out the significance of students' sense of 'belongingness' to the academic environment, and studies on retention (e.g. Yorke, 1999; Yorke and Longden, 2008: 26) have pointed to the deleterious effect of its obverse, isolation. It is challenging to develop a sense of belongingness among student cohorts which can include students who are mature and young, home-based or international, have varying entry qualifications and aptitudes, and have differing motivations for enrolling. Belongingness is associated with the culture of the section of the institution in which students are studying, the opportunities for social interaction, and friendship formation. The last two were found to be closely associated with positive course perceptions in students' first year and often lay the foundations for peer support in learning groups in the second year (see Chapter 6). Pedagogy can play a constructive part here, through teaching methods that encourage students to work with each other.

Step or slope?

The Framework for Higher Education Qualifications (FHEQ) in (most of) the UK and cognate frameworks elsewhere point to shifts of emphasis as students progress through the levels or years of their programmes. The step-up from the first to the second year is particularly evident where the first year is primarily concerned with students coming to terms with expectations that are different from school or other experiences. It is also evident, implicitly, where marks for the second year begin to 'count' towards the honours degree classification – though where they do not count in this way the students nevertheless have to pass the requisite number of first-year credits in order to progress (and eventually gain the desired qualification). However, when it comes to progression in learning, the metaphor of the step is less persuasive. In Chapter 2, curriculum design was presented more in terms of a spiral, in which learning became progressively wider and deeper – not always smoothly and at times quite jerkily. In terms of ascent, the step might be seen instead as a section of a rather rough pathway up a mountain.

Curriculum issues

Institutional processes relating to the design and implementation of curricula, such as aligning curricula with qualifications frameworks, auditing the curricula and monitoring the effects of implementation, should apply *a fortiori* to the second year because of the relative lack of definition noted in Chapter 2 and because of the shifts in students' perspectives recorded in Chapter 3. This is easy – indeed, obvious – to say, but more difficult in practice because the frameworks against which curricula are expected to be aligned are problematic.

If the 'big picture' logic of the spiral curriculum is followed through, even allowing for some freestanding modules and students' options that lie outside mainstream programmes, there is a tension between spirality and the stage levels laid out in qualifications frameworks. The problem is that qualifications frameworks are doing two things simultaneously:

a   providing statements of 'achievement level' that are helpful in defining awards at different stage points (e.g. Certificate, Diploma and Degree);
b   being taken by curriculum designers to provide guidance regarding learner development.

The first can be seen in terms of the espoused theory (Argyris and Schön, 1974) of qualifications frameworks, while the second constitutes a gloss on top of the first, more a matter of 'theory in use'. The problem with (b) can be exemplified through a consideration of 'criticality' which is widely accepted as a key aspect of student development in higher education and its appearance in the FHEQ (see Chapter 2).

In Table 8.1, criticality must be present in first-year higher education even though not explicitly mentioned since 'evaluation' very strongly implies it. ('Criticality' can, of course, be present in curricula that precede higher education.) Hence, criticality is relevant to all three levels of undergraduate education: what is different is the progressively greater range and complexity subsumed by the term as the student progresses through their programme and into life beyond.

Table 8.1 An extract from the Framework for Higher Education Qualifications (FHEQ)

FHEQ Level 4 (Year 1)	FHEQ Level 5 (Year 2)	FHEQ Level 6 (Year 3)
Evaluate approaches to problem solving	Use range of techniques and undertake critical analysis and interpretation.	Engage in critical evaluation and determine a solution or range of solutions to a problem.

The problem for the curriculum designer is to relate the linearity of qualification levels to the widening compass of criticality.

The spirality is schematically illustrated in Figure 8.1. The hexagons represent the six levels in Bloom's (1956) or Anderson and Krathwohl's (2001) cognitive taxonomies,[3] the numbering merely indicating the six. The hexagons become larger over time as learning develops (the assumption of progressive development is an ideal that does not always hold, of course: Kelly (1955) noted the possibility of a person repeating the same experience year after year without gaining significantly from it).

The challenge for the curriculum designer – and it is a severe one – is to find a way of describing the progressively widening compass of learning while being able to certify levels of achievement according to the FHEQ. It is also a challenge that national quality assurance agencies and international organisations need to take up.

Chapters 1 and 2 are where curriculum issues are primarily discussed.

Issue	Who might act
Defining the second year (middle years) so as to address the needs of both certification and progression in learning	Curriculum designers; institutional quality assurance personnel. At the level of the national system, quality assurance agencies. Also, international organisations involved in quality assurance

Data systems

Higher education has over the years been increasingly required to collect and present data, for both external and internal purposes. The case study of the University of Amsterdam (Chapter 7) shows how one institution has tackled systematically the challenge of collating data from a multiplicity of sources and making reports available to interested parties.

Elsewhere, data systems may have developed organically in response to impinging requirements, with the 'big picture' being missed. At a round table discussion convened by the Times Higher Education, the disconnection of data items was acknowledged (Parr, 2014: 22, as originally presented):

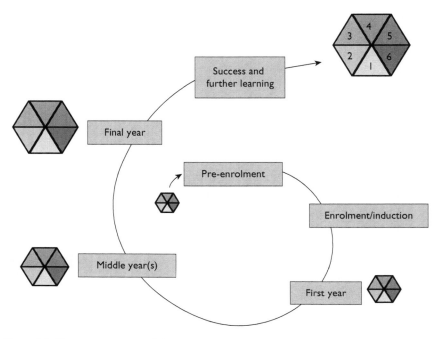

Figure 8.1 The growing span of the cognitive domain as students progress through higher education and develop in their lives beyond higher education

'Our data are fragmented', said Raftery.[4] As an example, he explained that if a student was late handing in essays on several courses, there was no guarantee that all of their tutors would be aware of the wider problem for the individual in question.

'There is something that we need to do about cohering that back-of-house [technology]', he added.

Red flags are going up but we don't know because we don't bring [this information] together.

Alison Allden, chief executive of the Higher Education Statistics Agency in the UK, noted in the same discussion that there was 'quite a lot of work to do in universities' to make their data systems capable of responding to the many demands being made of them (Parr, 2014: 22).

If Raftery and Allden are right, then key issues for institutions to consider are

• what data might be needed, by whom and when;
• how such data would be collected;
• how records in their various component parts can be brought together;

- who would have access to what data; and
- what analyses would be needed for which purposes and what audiences.

It would be important to involve all interested parties in developing an integrated information system and for the contributors to the development to acknowledge that practical considerations imply the need for some give and take regarding what can be accommodated. For the purposes of the issues covered in this book, this would involve a subset of these broad issues.

A corollary of having a data system is having the capacity to make full use of it. This implies an institutional research function (see Volkwein's, 1999, typology, Chapter 1) which can analyse data and report findings in a way appropriate to the audience. In addition, as the empirical work conducted for this book indicates, there is for some purposes the need to investigate relevant issues: as a further example, Horton, Tucker and Coates (2013) undertook an empirical investigation of interventions regarding student transition from Year 1 to Year 2 at the University of Northampton and found student outcomes that were more positive in their 'treatment group' than those from a cognate subject area where the intervention was not implemented.

Whereas specific institutional research offices have long been established in US higher education institutions, elsewhere the institutional research function has tended to be dispersed among a variety of organisational units (Huisman, Hoekstra and Yorke, forthcoming). Whatever the organisational structure relating to institutional research, it is important that analyses are both timely and readily intelligible to the intended audience. Timeliness may require the use of analytical methods that are approximate rather than exact – for example, preparing cross-sectional analyses of quasi-cohorts instead of waiting for longitudinal data to capture a cohort's trajectory in the institution (Yorke and Zaitseva, 2013). Intelligibility may require the suppression of the finer details of statistical reporting in order for 'the message' of the analysis to be readily understood. In both cases, the concept of 'good enough' plays an important role.

Data-related issues are discussed in Chapter 7.

Issue	Who might act
Developing the institutional data system	Institutional leaders in conjunction with interested parties across the institution
Data analysis and presentation	Institutional researchers or others with relevant responsibilities

Culture

Putting together all the evidence collected in writing this book, one overarching issue becomes apparent – the culture of the institution and its component parts. This is transmitted, both explicitly and implicitly, in the signals that are sent to students. The higher education system and wider society place significant weight on indicators of performance, such as students' marks and degree classifications. The danger is that the indicators are treated, not as proxies, but as objective measures of student learning. To seek the highest scores on indicators is to parallel a student's commitment to performance goals: good student learning may be a consequence, but will not necessarily follow. An institutional commitment to students' (and its own) learning, if successfully implemented, is very likely to produce indicator scores that will satisfy external expectations.

Those in leadership roles across the higher education sector have a key responsibility for establishing and maintaining the culture of the institution. President Bill Clinton famously had on his desk a reminder reading 'IT'S THE ECONOMY, STUPID'. Leaders in higher education institutions might keep on their desks a similar reminder regarding their institution's culture.

Notes

1 See http://www.mnsu.edu/students/sophomores/.
2 Foundation degrees are two-year, full-time (or part-time equivalent) programmes in higher education which focus heavily on workplace experience. They span Levels 4 and 5 of the Framework for Higher Education Qualifications (FHEQ), and can be 'topped up' to an honours degree (Level 6).
3 A similar schema could be developed for the affective and psychomotor domains, but is not necessary for this discussion.
4 John Raftery, the then pro vice-chancellor, Student Experience, at Oxford Brookes University and now vice-chancellor, London Metropolitan University.

References

Akgun, S. and Ciarrochi, J. (2003). Learned resourcefulness moderates the relationship between academic stress and academic performance. *Educational Psychology, 23*(3), 287–94.

Ames, C. (1992). Classrooms: Goals, structures and student motivation. *Journal of Educational Psychology, 84,* 261–71.

Anderman, E. and Midgley, C. (1997). Changes in achievement goal orientations, perceived academic competence, and grades across the transition to middle-level school. *Contemporary Educational Psychology, 22,* 269–98.

Anderson, L. W. and Krathwohl, D. R. (Eds.). (2001). *A taxonomy for learning, teaching, and assessing: A revision of Bloom's Taxonomy of Educational Objectives.* Boston, MA: Allyn & Bacon (Pearson Education Group).

Andrews, B. and Wilding, J. M. (2004). The relation of depression and anxiety to life-stress and achievement in students. *British Journal of Psychology, 95,* 509–21.

Argyris, C. and Schön, D. (1974). *Theory in practice: Increasing professional effectiveness.* San Francisco, CA: Jossey-Bass.

Atkinson, J. W. (1964). *An introduction to motivation.* Princeton, NJ: Van Nostrand.

Australian Education Council: Mayer Committee. (1992). *Key competencies: Report of the Committee to advise the Australian Education Council and Ministers of Vocational Education, Employment and Training on employment-related key competencies for postcompulsory education and training* (The Mayer Report). Canberra: Australian Government Publishing Service.

Baker, S. (2003). A prospective longitudinal investigation of social problem-solving appraisals on adjustment to university, stress, health and academic motivation and performance. *Personality and Individual Differences, 35,* 569–91.

Bandura, A. (1997). *Self-efficacy: The exercise of control.* New York: Freeman.

Baxter Magolda, M. (1992). *Knowing and reasoning in college.* San Francisco, CA: Jossey-Bass.

Baxter Magolda, M. (2009). Educating students for self-authorship: Learning partnerships to achieve complex outcomes. In C. Kreber (Ed.), *The university and its disciplines: Teaching and learning within and beyond disciplinary boundaries.* Abingdon: Routledge, 143–56.

Bean, J. P. and Eaton, S. B. (2000). A psychological model of college student retention. In J. M. Braxton (Ed.), *Reworking the student departure puzzle.* Nashville, TN: Vanderbilt University Press, 48–61.

Beard, C., Clegg, S. and Smith, K. (2007). Acknowledging the affective in higher education. *British Educational Research Journal*, 33(2), 235–52.

Bloom, B. S. (1956). *Taxonomy of educational objectives, Handbook 1: Cognitive domain*. London: Longman.

Blundell, R., Dearden, L., Goodman, A. and Reed, H. (2000). The returns to higher education in Britain: Evidence from a British cohort. *The Economic Journal*, 110(461), F82–99.

Bond, L. (2009). *Toward informative assessment and a culture of evidence* (A Report from Strengthening Pre-collegiate Education in Community Colleges). Stanford, CA: The Carnegie Foundation for the Advancement of Teaching.

Booth, A. (2005). *Worlds in collision: University tutor and student perspectives on the transition to degree level history.* At: http://sas-space.sas.ac.uk/4336/1/Worlds_in_collision_university_tutor_and_student_perspectives_on_the_transition_to_degree_level_history.pdf (retrieved 1 June 2014).

Bowles, A., Dobson, A., Fisher, R. and McPhail, R. (2011). An exploratory investigation into first year student transition to university. In K. Krause, M. Buckridge, C. Grimmer and S. Purbrick-Illek (Eds.), *Research and development in higher education: Reshaping higher education*. Milperra, Australia: Higher Education Research and Development Society of Australasia, 61–71.

Bråten, I. and Olaussen, O. (2005). Profiling individual differences in student motivation: A longitudinal cluster-analytic study in different academic contexts. *Contemporary Educational Psychology*, 30, 359–96.

Brennan, J., Durazzi, N. and Séné, T. (2013). *Things we know and don't know about the wider benefits of higher education: A review of the recent literature* (BIS Research Paper Number 133). London: Department for Business Innovation and Skills.

Broecke, S. and Nicholls, T. (2007). *Ethnicity and degree attainment* (DFES Research Report RW92). At: http://webarchive.nationalarchives.gov.uk/2013 0401151715/https://www.education.gov.uk/publications/eOrderingDownload/RW92.pdf (retrieved 23 May 2014).

Brooman, S. and Darwent, S. (2013). Measuring the beginning: A quantitative analysis of the transition to higher education. *Studies in Higher Education*. At: http://dx.doi.org/10.1080/03075079.2013.801428 (retrieved 3 June 2014).

Bruinsma, M. (2004). Motivation, cognitive processing and achievement in higher education. *Learning and Instruction*, 14(6), 549–68.

Bruner, J. (1960). *The process of education*. Cambridge, MA: Harvard University Press.

Bynner, J., Dolton, P., Feinstein, L., Makepeace, G., Malmberg, L. and Woods, L. (2003). *Revisiting the benefits of higher education*. Bristol: Higher Education Funding Council for England. At: http://dera.ioe.ac.uk/5167/ (retrieved 24 May 2014).

Bynner, J. and Egerton, M. (2001). *The wider benefits of higher education* (Report 01/46). Bristol: Higher Education Funding Council for England. At: http://dera.ioe.ac.uk/5993/ (retrieved 24 May 2014).

Cabrera, A. F., Nora, A. and Castaneda, M. B. (1993). College persistence: Structural equations modeling test of an integrated model of student retention. *The Journal of Higher Education*, 64(2), 123–39.

Carless, D. (2007). Learning-oriented assessment: Conceptual bases and practical implications. *Innovations in Education and Teaching International*, 44, 57–66.

Carnevale, A. P. and Strohl, J. (2013). *Separate and unequal: How higher education reinforces intergenerational reproduction of white privilege.* Washington, DC: Center on Education and the Workforce, Georgetown Public Policy Institute.

Center for Community College Student Engagement. (2014). *Aspirations to achievement: Men of color and community colleges.* Austin, TX: Center for Community College Student Engagement, University of Texas at Austin.

Chemers, M., Hu, L. and Garcia, B. (2001). Academic self-efficacy and first-year college student performance and adjustment. *Journal of Educational Psychology, 93*(1), 55–64.

Chickering, A. and Reisser, L. (1993). *Education and identity* (2nd ed.). San Francisco, CA, Jossey-Bass.

Chickering, A. W. and Gamson, Z. F. (1987). Seven principles for good practice in undergraduate education. *American Association of Higher Education Bulletin, 39*(7), 3–7.

Childs, P. and Spencer, J. (2002). *Autonomy and the ability to learn: Making the transition to higher education.* York: Higher Education Academy, UK Centre for Legal Education.

Christie, H., Munro, M. and Wager, F. (2005). 'Day students' in higher education: Widening access students and successful transitions to university life'. *International Studies in Sociology of Education, 15*(1), 3–29.

Church, M., Elliot, A. and Gable, S. (2001). Perceptions of classroom environment, achievement goals and achievement outcomes. *Journal of Educational Psychology, 93*, 43–54.

Ciani, K. D., Sheldon, K. M., Hilpert, J. C. and Easter, M. A. (2011). Antecedents and trajectories of achievement goals: A self-determination theory perspective. *British Journal of Educational Psychology, 81*, 223–43.

Cohen, S., Kamarck, T. and Mermelstein, R. (1983). A global measure of perceived stress. *Journal of Health and Social Behavior, 24*, 385–96.

Cordova, D. I. and Lepper, M. R. (1996). Intrinsic motivation and the process of learning: Beneficial effects of contextualization, personalization and choice. *Journal of Educational Psychology, 88*(4), 715–30.

Corkin, D. M., Yu, S. L. and Lindt, S. F. (2011). Comparing active delay and procrastination from a self-regulated learning perspective. *Learning and Individual Differences, 21*, 602–6.

Cousin, G., Hammond, N., Masterson, J., Sin, C., Dandridge, N., Rawat, S. and Williams, J. (2008). *Ethnicity, gender and degree attainment project: Final report.* York: Higher Education Academy.

Credé, M. and Phillips, A. (2011). A meta-analytic review of the Motivated Strategies for Learning Questionnaire. *Learning and Individual Differences, 21*, 337–46.

Crisp, G. T. (2011). Integrative assessment: Reframing assessment practice for current and future learning. *Assessment & Evaluation in Higher Education, 37*, 33–43.

Daniels, L. M., Frenzel, A. C., Stupnisky, R. H., Stewart, T. L. and Perry, R. P. (2013). Personal goals as predictors of intended classroom goals: Comparing elementary and secondary school pre-service teachers. *British Journal of Educational Psychology, 83*(3), 396–413.

Darwent, S. (2011). *Exploring the impact of a group-based intervention on first-year law students' self-efficacy, autonomous learning and social integration into university* (Dissertation for Masters in Research). Liverpool John Moores University.

Darwent, S. and Stewart, M. (2014). *Are student characteristics implicated in the 'sophomore slump'?* Second Year Experience Project Report. At: http://secondyearexperience.ljmu.ac.uk/?page_id=1040 (retrieved 9 June 2014).

Davies R. and Elias P. (2003). *Dropping out: A study of early leavers from higher education* (Research Report 386). London: Department for Education and Skills.

Dearing, R. (1997). *Higher education in the learning society. The report of the National Committee of Inquiry into Higher Education* (The Dearing Report). At: www.leeds.ac.uk/educol/ncihe (retrieved 27 May 2014).

Deci, E. L. and Ryan, R. M. (1985). *Intrinsic motivation and self-determination in human behavior.* New York: Plenum.

De Clercq, M., Galand, B. and Frenay, M. (2013). Chicken or the egg: Longitudinal analysis of the causal dilemma between goal orientation, self-regulation and cognitive processing strategies in higher education. *Studies in Educational Evaluation, 39*, 4–13.

Department for Education and Skills. (2002). *Success-for all: Reforming further education and training.* London: HMSO.

Department for Education and Skills. (2003). *The future of higher education.* Norwich: The Stationery Office.

Dodgson, M., Middleton, S., Rooney, D. and Cretchley, J. (2008). *Content analysis of submissions by Leximancer.* At: http://www.industry.gov.au/science/policy/Pages/Library%20Card/LeximancerSubmissionAnalysis.aspx (retrieved 1 June 2014).

Dweck, C. S. and Elliott, E. S. (1983). Achievement motivation. In P. Mussen and E. M. Hetherington (Eds.), *Handbook of child psychology.* New York: Wiley, 643–91.

Elliot, A. and McGregor, H. (2001). A 2 × 2 achievement goal framework. *Journal of Personality and Social Psychology, 80*(3), 501–9.

Equality Challenge Unit. (2012). *Equality in higher education: Statistical report 2012* (Part 2: Students). At: http://www.ecu.ac.uk/publications/equality-in-he-stats-2012/ (retrieved 23 May 2014).

Evans, C., Kirby, J. and Fabrigar, L. (2003). Approaches to learning, need for cognition, and strategic flexibility among university students. *British Journal of Educational Psychology, 73*, 507–28.

Evans, G., Nash, M., Nguyen, A., Nichol, E., Sillitoe, J. and Webb, J. (1999, September 26–29). *Student perspectives: The second year blues.* Paper presented at the 11th Annual Conference and Convention of the Australasian Association for Engineering Education, Adelaide.

Ewell, P. T. and Jones, D. P. (1994). Pointing the way: Indicators as policy tools in higher education. In S. S. Ruppert (Ed.), *Charting higher education accountability: A sourcebook on state-level performance indicators.* Denver, CO: Education Commission of the States, 6–16.

Fazey, D. M. A. and Fazey, J. A. (2001). The potential for autonomy in learning: Perceptions of competence, motivation and locus of control in first-year undergraduate students. *Studies in Higher Education, 26*(3), 345–61.

Fisher, R., Raines, P. and Burns, T. (2011). *The sophomore-year experience* (Proposed Quality Enhancement Plan). Belmont University. At: www.belmont.edu/institutional_effectiveness/pdfs/stc-qep.pdf (retrieved 24 May 2014).

Flanagan, J. (1954). The critical incident technique. *Psychological Bulletin, 51*(4), 377–58.

Freedman, M. B. (1956). The passage through college. *Journal of Social Issues, 12*, 13–27.

Furr, S. and Gannoway, L. (1982). Easing the sophomore slump: A student development approach. *Journal of College Student Personnel, 23*, 340–41.

Gahagan, J. and Hunter, M. S. (2006). The second-year experience: Turning attention to the academy's middle children. *About Campus, 11*, 17–22.

Gibbs, G. (1999). Using assessment strategically to change the way students learn. In S. Brown and A. Glasner (Eds.), *Assessment matters in higher education*. Buckingham: SRHE and Open University Press, 41–53.

Gibbs, G. and Simpson, C. (2005). Conditions under which assessment supports learning. *Learning and Teaching in Higher Education, 1*, 3–31.

Graunke, S. S. and Woosley, S. A. (2005). An exploration of factors that affect the academic success of college sophomores. *College Student Journal, 39*(2), 367–76.

Gump, S. E. (2007). Classroom research in a general education course: Exploring implications through an investigation of the sophomore slump. *Journal of General Education, 56*(2), 105–25.

Haarala-Muholen, A., Ruohoniemi, M., Katajauori, N. and Lindblom-Ylänne, S. (2011). Comparison of students' perceptions of their teaching-learning environments in three professional academic disciplines: A valuable tool for quality enhancement. *Learning Environments Research, 14*, 155–69.

Haggis, T. (2006). Pedagogies for diversity: Retaining critical challenge amidst fears of 'dumbing down'. *Studies in Higher Education, 31*(5), 521–35.

Harackiewicz, J., Barron, K., Tauer, J. and Elliot, A. (2002). Predicting success in college: A longitudinal study of achievement goals and ability measures as predictors of interest and performance from freshman year through graduation. *Journal of Educational Psychology, 94*(3), 562–75.

Higher Education Academy. (2008). *Strategic plan 2008–13*. York: Higher Education Academy.

Higher Education Funding Council for England. (2001). *Strategies for widening participation in higher education: A guide to good practice*. Bristol: Higher Education Funding Council for England.

Higher Education Funding Council for England. (2003). *Schooling effects on higher education achievement*. At: http://webarchive.nationalarchives.gov.uk/2012011817 1947/http://www.hefce.ac.uk/pubs/hefce/2003/03_32.htm (retrieved May 2014).

Higher Education Funding Council for England. (2005). *Schooling effects on higher education achievement: Further analysis – Entry at 19*. At: http://webarchive. nationalarchives.gov.uk/20120118171947/http://www.hefce.ac.uk/pubs/ hefce/2005/05_09/ (retrieved 27 May 2014).

Higher Education Funding Council for England. (2014). *Differences in degree outcomes: Key findings*. At: https://www.hefce.ac.uk/pubs/year/2014/201403/ name,86821,en.html (retrieved 1 June 2014).

Hoekstra, J. P. (2005). Institutional research in de Lage Landen. Een geschiedenis. In V. Vendel and M. Korsten (Eds.), *Institutional research in het hoger onderwijs, een abecedarium*. Amsterdam: Dutch Association for Institutional Research, 159–64.

Hoekstra, J. P. and Vendel, V. (1999). Customised performance indicators: Benchmarks of university education in the Netherlands. *Journal of Institutional Research in Australia, 8*(1), 8–16.

Horton, J., Tucker, F. and Coates, S. (2013). Supporting undergraduates' transitions to year 2: Banishing the "second-year blues". In R. Clark, J. Andrews, L. Thomas and R. Aggarwal (Eds.), *Compendium of effective practice in higher education* (Vol. 2). York: Higher Education Academy, 148–51.

Howe, M. J. A. (1974). The utility of taking notes as an aid to learning. *Educational Research, 16*(3), 222–27.

Huisman, J., Hoekstra, P. and Yorke, M. (forthcoming). Institutional research in Europe: A view from the European Association for Institutional Research. In A. Calderon and K. Webber (Eds.), *The global context of institutional research and planning in higher education.* TBA.

Hunter, M. S., Tobolowsky, B. F., Gardner, J. N., Evenbeck, S. E., Pattengale, J. A., Schaller, M. A., Schreiner, L. A. and associates. (2010). *Helping sophomores succeed: Understanding and improving the second-year experience.* San Francisco, CA: Jossey-Bass.

Institute for Higher Education Policy. (1998). *Reaping the benefits: Defining the public and private benefits of going to college.* Washington, DC: Institute for Higher Education Policy.

Jacobs, P. A. and Newstead, S. E. (2000). The nature and development of student motivation. *British Journal of Educational Psychology, 70*(2), 243–54.

James, R., Krause, K.-L. and Jennings, C. (2010). *The first year experience in Australian Universities: Findings from 1994 to 2009.* Centre for the Study of Higher Education, University of Melbourne. At www.cshe.unimelb.edu.au/research/FYE_Report_1994_to_2009.pdf (retrieved 1 June 2014)

James, W. (1900). *The principles of psychology* (Vol. 1). New York: Henry Holt and Co. (Reprinted 1950, New York: Dover).

Kaplan, A. and Maehr, M. (1999). Achievement goals and student wellbeing. *Contemporary Educational Psychology, 24,* 330–58.

Kelly, G. A. (1955). *The psychology of personal constructs* (2 Vols). New York: Norton.

Kimball, R. (1996). *The Data Warehouse Toolkit: Practical techniques for building dimensional data warehouses.* New York: John Wiley.

King, P. M. and Kitchener, K. S. (1994). *Developing reflective judgment: Understanding and promoting intellectual growth and critical thinking in adolescents and young adults.* San Francisco, CA: Jossey-Bass.

Kohlberg, L. (1964). *The philosophy of moral development: Moral stages and the idea of justice.* San Francisco, CA: Harper & Row.

Krathwohl, D. R. (2002). A revision of Bloom's Taxonomy: An overview. *Theory Into Practice, 41*(4), 212–18.

Kuhn, D. and Weinstock, M. (2002). What is epistemological thinking and why does it matter? In B. Hofer and P. Pintrich (Eds.), *Personal epistemology: The psychological beliefs about knowledge and knowing.* Mahwah, NJ: Lawrence Erlbaum, 121–44.

Lane, J. and Lane, A. (2001). Self-efficacy and academic performance. *Social Behavior and Personality, 29*(7), 687–94.

Lane, J., Lane, A. and Kyprianou, A. (2004). Self-efficacy, self-esteem and their impact on academic performance. *Social Behavior and Personality, 32*(3), 247–56.

Laycock, M. (2009). *Personal tutoring in higher education – Where now and where next? A literature review and recommendations* (SEDA Special 25). London: SEDA.

Leathwood, C. and O'Connell, P. (2003). 'It's a struggle': The construction of the 'new student' in higher education. *Journal of Education Policy, 18*(6), 597–615.

Leckey, J. and Cook, A. (1999). Do expectations meet reality? A survey of changes in first-year student opinion. *Journal of Further and Higher Education, 23*(2), 157–71.

Lee, E. (2005). The relationship of motivation and flow experience to academic procrastination in university students. *The Journal of Genetic Psychology, 166*, 5–15.

Lester, S. (2011). The UK qualifications and credit framework: A critique. *Journal of Vocational Education & Training, 63*(2), 205–16.

Lieberman, D. A. and Remedios, R. (2007). Do undergraduates' motives for studying change as they progress through their degrees? *British Journal of Educational Psychology, 77*(2), 379–95.

Lindsay, S. (2011). Do students in UK Higher Education Institutions need personal tutors? *Learning at City Journal, 1*(1), 40–45.

Locke, E. A., and Latham, G. P. (2002). Building a practically useful theory of goal setting and task motivation: A 35-year odyssey. *American Psychologist, 57*, 705–17.

Longden, B. (2002). Retention rates – Renewed interest but whose interest is being served? *Research Papers in Education, 17*(1), 3–29.

Macaskill, A. and Denovan, A. (2013). Developing autonomous learning in first year university students using perspectives from positive psychology. *Studies in Higher Education, 38*(1), 124–42.

Macaskill, A. and Taylor, E. (2010). The development of a brief measure of learner autonomy in university students. *Studies in Higher Education, 35*(3), 351–9.

McDowell, L., Wakelin, D., Montgomery, C. and King, S. (2011). Does assessment for learning make a difference? The development of a questionnaire to explore the student response. *Assessment & Evaluation in Higher Education, 36*(7), 749–65.

McIlroy, D. and Bunting, B. (2002). Personality, behavior and achievement: Principles for educators to inculcate and students to model. *Contemporary Educational Psychology, 27*, 326–37.

McInnis, C. (2001). Researching the first year experience: Where to from here? *Higher Education Research & Development, 20*(2), 105–14.

Maclellan, E. (2001). Assessment for learning: The differing perceptions of tutors and students. *Assessment & Evaluation in Higher Education, 26*(4), 307–18.

McQueen, H. (2009). Institution and regulation matters in educational transition: A theoretical critique of retention and attrition models. *British Journal of Educational Studies, 57*(1), 70–88.

Maguire, S. (2006). Induction as a longitudinal process. In A. Cook, B. S. Rushton and K. A. Macintosh (Eds.), *Supporting students: Extended induction* (Booklet Produced for the STAR Project). Coleraine: University of Ulster, 13–17.

Malau-Aduli, B., Page, W., Cooling, N. and Turner, R. (2013). Impact of self-efficacy beliefs on short- and long-term academic improvements for underperforming medical students. *American Journal of Educational Research, 1*(6), 168–76.

Marjanovic, O. (1999). Learning and teaching in a synchronous collaborative environment. *Journal of Computer Assisted Learning, 15*, 129–38.

Matthews, D. (2014, January). Poorer students present 'financial risk'. *The Times Higher Education*, pp. 6–7.

May, S. and Bousted, M. (2004). Investigation of student retention through an analysis of the first-year experience of students at Kingston University. *Widening Participation and Lifelong Learning, 6*(2), 42–48.

Mehaut, P. and Winch, C. (2012). The European qualification framework: Skills, competences or knowledge? *European Educational Research Journal, 11*(3), 369–81.

Miller, C. M. L. and Parlett, M. (1974). *Up to the mark: A study of the examination game*. Guildford: Society for Research into Higher Education.

Miller, R. H. (2014). *Avoiding the sophomore slump*. At: http://www.education. com/reference/article/avoiding-sophomore-slump/ (retrieved 24 May 2014).

Miller, T. E. (2005). Student persistence and degree attainment. In T. Miller, B. Bender, J. Schuh and Associates (Eds.), *Promoting reasonable expectations: Aligning student and institutional views of the college experience*. San Francisco, CA: Jossey-Bass, 122–39.

Moore, R. (1995). *Retention rates research project*. Sheffield: Sheffield Hallam University.

Morgan, M. and Brown, S. (2010). Commencement of the academic year: Welcoming, inducting and developing students. In S. Denton and S. Brown (Eds.), *A practical guide to university and college management: Beyond bureaucracy*. New York, NY: Routledge, 47–68.

Murray, J. (2009). The wider social benefits of higher education: What do we know about them? *Australian Journal of Education, 53*(3), 230–44.

Neville, L. (2007). *The personal Tutor's handbook*. Basingstokem: Palgrave Macmillan.

Nicholls, J. (1984). Conceptions of ability and achievement motivation. In R. Ames and C. Ames (Eds.), *Research on motivation in education: Student motivation* (Vol. 1). New York: Academic Press, 39–73.

Noel-Levitz. (2013). *2013 report: The attitudes of second-year college students – Exploring the mindsets behind the 'sophomore slump'*. At: https://www.noellevitz. com/papers-research-higher-education/2013/2013-report-the-attitudes-of-second-year-college-students (retrieved 25 May 2014).

Ordóñez, L. D., Schweiter, M. E., Galinsky, A. D. and Bazerman, M. H. (2009). Goals gone wild: The systematic side effects of over-prescribing goal setting. *Academy of Management Perspectives, 23*(1), 6–16.

Palmer, M., O'Kane, P. and Owens, M. (2009). Betwixt spaces: Student accounts of turning point experiences in the first year transition. *Studies in Higher Education, 34*(1), 37–54.

Parmar, D. (2004, September). *Building success for all our students: Enhancing the student experience*. Paper presented at the Improving Student Learning Conference 2004, Diversity and Inclusivity, Birmingham.

Parr, C. (2014). Competition gives new meaning to a nebulous notion. *THE Student Experience Survey 2014* [supplement to *Times Higher Education* No. 2152, 15–21 May], 22–23.

Pascarella, E. T. and Terenzini, P. T. (2005). *How college affects students: A third decade of research*. San Francisco, CA: Jossey-Bass.

Pattengale, J. and Schreiner, L. A. (2000). Policies and practices to enhance sophomore success. In L. A. Schreiner and J. Pattengale (Eds.), *Visible solutions for invisible students: Helping sophomores succeed* (Monograph No. 31). Columbia, SC: University of South Carolina, National Resource Center for the First-Year Experience and Students in Transition, v–vii.

Peat, M., Dalziel, J. and Grant, A. M. (2001). Enhancing the first year student experience by facilitating the development of peer networks through a one-day workshop. *Higher Education Research & Development, 20*(2), 199–215.

Peguesse, C. (2008). *Quality enhancement plan: Sophomore year experience program*. At: http://www.valdosta.edu/administration/sacs/qep/documents/ QEPProposalforSYE_000.pdf (retrieved 24 May 2014).

Penn-Edwards, S. (2010) Computer-aided phenomenography: The role of Leximancer computer software in phenomenographic investigation. *The Qualitative Report, 15*, 252–67.

Perry, W. G. (1998). *Forms of ethical and intellectual development in the college years.* San Francisco, CA: Jossey-Bass. (Reprint of 1970 text, with a new introduction by L.L. Knefelkamp)

Phan, H. (2009). Relations between goals, self-efficacy, critical thinking and deep processing strategies: A path analysis. *Educational Psychology: An International Journal of Experimental Educational Psychology, 29*(7), 777–99.

Piaget, J. (1929/2000). *The child's conception of the world* (tr. J. Tomlinson and A. Tomlinson). Savage, MD: Littlefield Adams.

Pintrich, P. R. (1999). The role of motivation in promoting and sustaining self-regulated learning. *International Journal of Educational Research, 31*(6), 459–70.

Pintrich, P. R. (2000). The role of goal orientation in self-regulated learning. In P. R. Pintrich and M. Zeidner (Eds.), *Handbook of self-regulation.* San Diego, CA: Academic Press, 451–502.

Pintrich, P. R. (2004). A conceptual framework for assessing motivation and self-regulated learning in college students. *Educational Psychology Review, 16*(4), 385–407.

Pintrich, P. R. and Schunk, D. H. (2002). *Motivation in education: Theory, research, and applications* (2nd ed.). Upper Saddle River, NJ: Prentice Hall.

Pintrich, P. R., Smith, D., Garcia, T. and McKeachie, W. (1993). Reliability and predictive validity of the Motivated Strategies for Learning Questionnaire (MSLQ). *Educational and Psychological Measurement, 53*, 801–13.

Pokorny, M. and Pokorny, H. (2005). Widening participation in higher education: Student quantitative skills and independent learning as impediments to progression. *International Journal of Mathematical Education in Science and Technology, 36*(5), 445–67.

Price, M., Handley, K., Millar, J. and O'Donovan, B. (2010). Feedback: All that effort, but what is the effect? *Assessment & Evaluation in Higher Education, 35*(3), 277–89.

Purcell, K., Elias, P., Atfield, G., Behle, H., Ellison, R., Luchinskaya, D., Snape, J., Conaghan, L. and Tzanakou, C. (2012). *Futuretrack stage 4: Transitions into employment, further study and other outcomes.* Coventry: Warwick Institute for Employment Research.

Quality Assurance Agency. (2008). *The framework for higher education qualifications in England, Wales and Northern Ireland.* At: http://www.qaa.ac.uk/publications/ information-and-guidance/publication?PubID=2718 (retrieved 18 August 2014).

Quality Assurance Agency. (2013). *UK quality code for higher education – Part A: Setting and maintaining academic standards.* At: http://www.qaa.ac.uk/ publications/information-and-guidance/publication?PubID=182 (retrieved 27 May 2014).

Raffe, D. (2011). Are "communications frameworks" more successful? Policy learning from the Scottish credit and qualifications framework. *Journal of Education and Work, 24*(3–4), 283–302.

Rainey, M. A. and Kolb, D. (1995). Using experiential learning theory and learning styles in diversity education. In R. R. Sims and S. J. Sims (Eds.), *The importance of learning styles: Understanding the implications for learning, course design and education.* Westport, CT: Greenwood Press, 129–46.

Ramsden, P. (1992). *Learning to teach in higher education.* London: Routledge.

Ranellucci, J., Muis, K., Duffy, M., Wang, X., Sampasivam, L. and Franco, G. (2013). To master or perform? Exploring relations between achievement goals and conceptual change learning. *British Journal of Educational Psychology, 83,* 431–51.

Remedios, R., Kiseleva, Z. and Elliott, J. (2008). Goal orientations in Russian university students: From mastery to performance? *Educational Psychology: An International Journal of Experimental Educational Psychology, 28*(6), 677–91.

Richardson, D. (2003). *The transition to degree level study* (Higher Education Academy Report). At: http://www.heacademy.ac.uk/assets/documents/resources/database/id506_transition_to_degree_level_study.pdf (retrieved 3 June 2014).

Richardson, D. (2004). *The transition to degree level study.* At: http://jisctechdis.ac.uk/assets/documents/resources/database/id506_transition_to_degree_level_study.pdf (retrieved 25 May 2014).

Rickinson, B. and Rutherford, D. (1995). Increasing undergraduate student retention rates. *British Journal of Guidance & Counselling, 23*(2), 161–72.

Robbins, S. K. (2006). Introducing PASS: The School of Biological and Molecular Sciences (BMS) Personal and Academic Support System: Supporting first year students within an academic School through pro-active Personal Tutoring. *Brookes eJournal of Learning and Teaching, 2*(1). At: http://bejlt.brookes.ac.uk/article/introducing_pass-2/ (retrieved 1 June 2014).

Robertson, D. (2002). *Intermediate-level qualifications in higher education: An international assessment.* At: http://webarchive.nationalarchives.gov.uk/20120118171947/http://www.hefce.ac.uk/pubs/rdreports/2002/rd10_02/ (retrieved 24 May 2014).

Rome, J. (2004). Development of data warehouse. In National Association of College and University Business Officers (Ed.), *Managerial analysis and decision support: A guidebook and case studies.* Washington, DC: National Association of College and University Business Officers.

Ruiz, S., Sharkness, J., Kelly, K., DeAngelo, L. and Pryor, J. (2010). *Findings from the 2009 administration of the Your First College Year (YFCY): National aggregates.* Higher Education Research Institute, University of California, Los Angeles.

Sadler, D. R. (1987). Specifying and promulgating achievement standards. *Oxford Review of Education, 13*(2), 191–209.

Sadler, D. R. (1998). Formative assessment: Revisiting the territory. *Assessment & Evaluation in Higher Education, 5*(1), 77–84.

Sanchez-Leguelinel, C. (2008). Supporting 'slumping' sophomores: Programmatic peer initiatives designed to enhance retention in the crucial second year of college. *College Student Journal, 42*(2), 637–46.

Saupe, J. (1990). *The functions of institutional research* (2nd ed.). Tallahassee, FL: The Association for Institutional Research.

Schaller, M. (2005). Traversing the uneven terrain of the second college year. *About Campus, 10,* 17–24.

Scott, J. and Cashmore, A. (2012). *Fragmented transitions: Moving to the 2nd year.* At: http://www.heacademy.ac.uk/assets/documents/stem-conference/BioSciences1/Jon_Scott.pdf (retrieved 25 May 2014).

Serban, A. M. (2002). Knowledge management: The fifth face of institutional research. In A. M. Serban and J. Luan (Eds.), *Knowledge management: Building a competitive advantage in higher education* (New Directions for Institutional Research, No. 113). San Francisco, CA: Jossey-Bass, 105–11.

Sheard, M. and Golby, J. (2007). Hardiness and undergraduate academic study: The moderating role of commitment. *Personality and Individual Differences, 43,* 579–88.

Simon, H. A. (1957). *Models of man.* New York: Wiley.

Simons, J., Dewitte, S. and Lens, W. (2004). The role of different types of instrumentality in motivation, study strategies and performance: Know why you learn, so you'll know what you learn! *British Journal of Educational Psychology, 74,* 343–60.

Slavin, R. E. (1996). Research for the future: Research on cooperative learning and achievement: What we know, what we need to know. *Contemporary Educational Psychology, 21*(1), 43–69.

Smith, A. and Humphreys, M. (2006). Evaluation of unsupervised semantic mapping of natural language with Leximancer concept mapping, language with Leximancer concept mapping. *Behavior Research Methods, 38,* 262–79.

Smith, K., Davy, J. and Rosenberg, D. (2012). An empirical analysis of an alternative configuration of the Academic Motivation Scale. *Assessment in Education, 19*(2), 231–50.

Smyth, J., Hockemeyer, J., Heron, K., Wonderlich, S. and Pennebaker, J. (2008). Prevalence, type, disclosure and severity of adverse life events in college students. *Journal of American College Health, 57*(1), 69–76.

Snyder, B. R. (1971). *The hidden curriculum.* New York: Knopf.

Soilemetzidis, I., Bennett, P., Buckley, A., Hillman, N. and Stoakes, G. (2014). *The HEPI–HEA Student Academic Experience Survey 2014.* York: Higher Education Academy and Higher Education Policy Institute.

Steel, P. (2007). The nature of procrastination: A meta-analytical and theoretical review of quintessential self-regulatory failure. *Psychological Bulletin, 133,* 65–94.

Stewart, M., Stott, T. A. and Nuttall, A.-M. (in press). Students' study goals & procrastination tendencies at different stages of the undergraduate degree. *Studies in Higher Education.*

Strick, C. and Creagh, N. (2008). *Making your data work for you: Data quality and efficiency in higher education* (Price Waterhouse Coopers Report to HEFCE, HEFCW, HESA, SFC and TDAS) London: Price Waterhouse Coopers.

Struthers, C., Perry, R. and Menec, V. (2000). An examination of the relationship amongst academic stress, coping, motivation and performance in college. *Research in Higher Education, 41*(5), 581–92.

Terenzini, P. (1993). On the nature of institutional research and the knowledge and skills it requires. *Research in Higher Education, 34*(1), 1–10.

Terenzini, P. T., Rendon, L., Upcraft, L., Millar, S., Allison, K., Gregg, P. and Jalomo, R. (1994). The transition to college: Diverse students, diverse stories. *Research in Higher Education, 35*(1), 57–73.

Thomas, L. (2011). Do pre-entry interventions such as 'Aimhigher' impact on student retention and success? A review of the literature. *Higher Education Quarterly, 65*(3), 230–50.

Thomas, L. (2012). *Building student engagement and belonging in higher education at a time of change: Final report from the what works? Student Retention & Success programme.* London: Paul Hamlyn Foundation.

Thomas, L. and Hixenbaugh, P. (Eds.). (2006). *Personal tutoring in higher education.* Stoke-on-Trent: Trentham Books.

Tight, M. (2007). Bridging the divide: A comparative analysis of articles in higher education journals published inside and outside North America. *Higher Education, 53*(2), 235–53.

Tinto, V. (1993). *Leaving college: Rethinking the causes and cures of student attrition* (2nd ed.). Chicago, IL: University of Chicago Press.

Tinto, V. (1994). *Leaving college: Rethinking the causes and cures of student attrition* (2nd ed.). Chicago, IL: University of Chicago.

Tinto, V. (1997). Classrooms as communities: Exploring the educational character of student persistence. *The Journal of Higher Education, 68*, 599–623.

Tobolowsky, B. F. (2008). Sophomores in transition: The forgotten year. In B. O. Barefoot (Ed.), *The first year and beyond: Rethinking the challenge of collegiate transition* (New Directions for Higher Education, No. 144). San Francisco, CA: Jossey-Bass, 59–67.

Tobolowsky, B. F. and Cox, B. E. (2007). *Shedding light on sophomores: An exploration of the second college year* (Monograph No. 47). Columbia, SC: University of South Carolina, National Resource Center for the First-Year Experience and Students in Transition.

Trigwell, K., Ashwin, P. and Millan, E. S. (2013). Evoked prior learning experience and approach to learning as predictors of academic achievement. *British Journal of Educational Psychology, 83*, 363–78.

Tuckman, B. W. (1991). The development and concurrent validity of the Procrastination Scale. *Educational and Psychological Measurement, 5*, 473–80.

Twenty-First Century Workforce Commission. (2000). *A nation of opportunity: Building America's 21st century workforce.* Washington, DC: Twenty-First Century Workforce Commission.

Tyrer, G., Dray, T., Ives, J. and Yorke, M. (2013). *Professional capabilities in non-vocational subject disciplines.* At: http://www.heacademy.ac.uk/resources/detail/employability/Professional-capabilities (retrieved 23 May 2014).

Vaez, M. and Laflamme, L. (2008). Experienced stress, psychological symptoms, self-related health and academic achievement: A longitudinal study of Swedish university students. *Social Behaviour and Personality, 36*(2), 183–96.

Vermetten, Y. J., Lodewijks, H. G. and Vermunt, J. D. (2001). The role of personality traits and goal orientations in strategy use. *Contemporary Educational Psychology, 26*(2), 149–70.

Volkwein, J. F. (1999). The four faces of institutional research. In J. F. Volkwein (Ed.), What is institutional research all about? A critical and comprehensive assessment of the profession (New Directions for Institutional Research, No. 104). San Francisco, CA: Jossey-Bass, 9–19.

Volkwein, J. F. (2008). The foundations and evolution of institutional research. In D. G. Terkla (Ed.), *Institutional research: More than just data* (New Directions for Higher Education, No.141). San Francisco, CA: Jossey-Bass, 5–20.

Vrugt, A. and Oort, F. (2008). Metacognition, achievement goals, study strategies and academic achievement: Pathways to achievement. *Metacognition Learning, 30*, 123–46.

Vygotsky, L. S. (1978). *Mind in society: The development of higher psychological processes.* Cambridge, MA: Harvard University Press.

Wäschle, K., Allgaier, A., Lachner, A., Fink, S. and Nückles, M. (2014). Procrastination and self-efficacy: Tracing vicious and virtuous circles in self-regulated learning. *Learning & Instruction, 29*, 103–14.

Weko, T. (2004). *New dogs and old tricks: What can the UK teach the US about university education?* At: http://www.hepi.ac.uk/wp-content/uploads/2014/02/11New-Dogs-and-Old-Tricks-What-Can-The-UK-Teach-the-US-about-University-Education-.pdf (retrieved 24 May 2014).

Whitchurch, C. (2008). *Professional managers in higher education: Preparing for complex futures final report.* London: Leadership Foundation for Higher Education.

White, J., Williams, R. W. and Green, B. F. (1999). Discontinuation, leaving reasons and course evaluation comments of students on the common foundation programme. *Nurse Education Today, 19*(2), 142–50.

Whittaker, R. (2008). *Quality enhancement themes: The first year experience – Transition to and during the first year.* Mansfield: The Quality Assurance Agency for Higher Education.

Wilcox, B. L. (1981). Social support, life stress, and psychological adjustment: A test of the buffering hypothesis. *American Journal of Community Psychology, 9,* 371–86.

Wilcox, P., Winn, S. and Fyvie-Gauld, M. (2005). It was nothing to do with the university, it was just the people: The role of social support in the first year experience of higher education. *Studies in Higher Education, 30*(6), 707–22.

Willcoxson, L., Cotter, J. and Joy, S. (2011). Beyond the first-year experience: The impact on attrition of student experiences throughout the undergraduate degree studies in six diverse universities. *Studies in Higher Education, 36*(3), 331–52.

Wilson, C. (2013). Supporting the transition of foundation degree students from levels 4 to 5. In R. Clark, J. Andrews, L. Thomas and R. Aggarwal (Eds.), *Compendium of effective practice in higher education* (Vol. 2). York: Higher Education Academy, 25–27.

Wolters, C. A. (2003). Understanding procrastination from a self-regulated learning perspective. *Journal of Educational Psychology, 95,* 179–87.

Wolters, C. A. (2004). Advancing achievement goal theory: Using goal structures and goal orientations to predict students' motivation, cognition and achievement. *Journal of Educational Psychology, 96,* 236–50.

Yorke, M. (1995). Taking the odds-on chance: Using performance indicators in managing for the improvement of quality in higher education. *Tertiary Education and Management, 1*(1), 49–57.

Yorke, M. (1999). *Leaving early: Undergraduate non-completion in higher education.* London: Falmer.

Yorke, M. (2006). Gold in them there hills? Extracting and using data from existing sources. *Tertiary Education and Management, 12*(3), 201–13.

Yorke, M. (2008). *Grading student achievement in higher education: Signals and shortcomings.* London: Routledge.

Yorke, M. (2011). Analysing existing datasets: Some considerations arising from practical experience. *International Journal of Research & Method in Education, 34*(3), 255–67.

Yorke, M., Barnett, G., Evanson, P., Haines, C., Jenkins, D., Knight, P., Scurry, D., Stowell, M. and Woolf, H. (2005). Mining institutional datasets to support policy making and implementation. *Journal of Higher Education and Policy Management, 27,* 285–98.

Yorke, M. and Longden, B. (2004). *Retention and student success in higher education.* Maidenhead: SRHE and Open University Press.

Yorke, M. and Longden, B. (2007). *The first-year experience in higher education in the UK: Report on phase 1 of a project funded by the Higher Education Academy.* York: Higher Education Academy.

Yorke, M. and Longden, B. (2008). *The first-year experience of higher education in the UK: Final report.* York: Higher Education Academy.

Yorke, M. and Zaitseva, E. (2013). Do cross-sectional student assessment data make a reasonable proxy for longitudinal data? *Assessment & Evaluation in Higher Education, 38*(8), 957–67.

Young, A. (1997). I think, therefore I'm motivated: The relations among cognitive strategy use, motivational orientation and classroom perceptions over time. *Learning and Individual Differences, 9,* 249–83.

Zaitseva, E., Milsom, C. and Stewart, M. (2013). Connecting the dots: Using concept maps for interpreting student satisfaction. *Quality in Higher Education, 19*(2), 225–47.

Zusho, A., Pintrich, P. R. and Coppola, B. (2003). Skill and will: The role of motivation and cognition in the learning of college chemistry. *International Journal of Science Education, 25,* 1081–94.

Index

Wäschle, K. 46, 128
wastage; *see* dropout
weighting: in Leximancer 26, 34–5; of
  marks 5–6, 66, 74, 109
Weinstock, M. 15, 122
Whitchurch, C. 81, 129
White, J. 81, 129
Whittaker, R. 68, 82, 129
widening participation 68, 82, 102
Wilcox, B.L. 77, 129
Wilcox, P. 28, 129
Wilding, J.M. 48, 117
Willcoxson, L. 50, 129
Wilson, C. 106, 129
Winch, C. 18, 123

withdrawal 50, 78
Wolters, C.A. 45–6, 64, 129
Woosley, S.A. 2–4, 6, 121
work/workplace experience 61–2, 72,
  78, 116
workload 12, 25, 30, 37, 39, 41, 46, 48,
  52–3, 57, 60–1, 63–4, 66, 70, 108

Yorke, M. 4, 7, 9–10, 13, 28, 66, 82, 86,
  92, 101–2, 111, 115, 122, 129, 130
Young, A. 64, 130

Zaitseva, E. 25, 38, 85–6, 115, 130
Zone of Proximal Development 77
Zusho, A. 41, 130

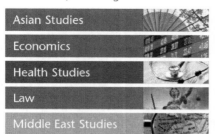

Printed by PGSTL